WI

# Consumer Collections and Recoveries: Operations and Strategies

**2nd Edition**

EDITED BY
MURRAY BAILEY

Published by

White Box Publishing
291 New Cheltenham Road
Kingswood
Bristol BS15 4RD

Trademarks
Many words in this publication that the authors and publisher believe to be trademarks, have been designated as such by use of initial capital letters. In so designating or failing to designate such words, neither the authors nor the publisher intends to express any judgment on the validity or legal status of any proprietary right that may be claimed in the words.

ISBN 0 - 9540053 - 2 - 5

## About INFORMA

INFORMA was founded in 1996 as a credit scoring company with the mission to help companies to get the most value out of data. INFORMA has grown strongly and is today the leading credit scoring company in Central Europe with clients in 12 countries in the banking, insurance, retail and telecom sectors.

In its core business of credit scoring, INFORMA's clients include the leading banks in Germany and Switzerland and it is the scoring supplier to the entire Savings Banks organisation with over 500 regional banks and 50% of the German retail banking business.

INFORMA's credit-score family, marketed as the INFORMA-Score, is used by hundreds of companies to predict the financial potential of applicants and customers and to optimise mailing lists.

INFORMA provides consulting services, helping companies to improve their decision processes in application processing, customer value management and revenue collection, as well as helping companies to find and implement software solutions that best solve their problems in all three areas.

INFORMA serves its clients from its offices in Germany. For more information on INFORMA Unternehmensberatung GmbH please visit www.informa.de or contact Dr. Paul Triggs on +49 611 97 85 0 or ptriggs@informa.de.


## About Talgentra

Talgentra is a global IT solutions company providing proven customer management, billing and revenue collection systems. Talgentra's solutions are deployed in utilities, communications, financial services, aerospace and the public sector.

Talgentra has secured a high profile international market presence with the Gentrack billing and customer management suite, the Tallyman credit management and collections solution, and Airport 20/20, an integrated airport management and billing system.

Talgentra's well established customer base, supported by a wide range of professional services and skills, includes many large, well known national and international companies in the UK, Southeast Asia and Australasia.

Talgentra is headquartered in the UK with offices in New Zealand, Australia, Singapore and Malaysia. Employing more than 200 people around the world, Talgentra is part of the Alchemy business portfolio which has more than £1 billion under investment, including a flourishing IT Group with sales of more than £300 million.

For more information on Talgentra please visit our website: www.Talgentra.com

## Acknowledgements

Thank you to all the authors who contributed to this book. Specifically I would like to thank the authors who obtained permission to contribute from their company. Donna Guest, Martyn Phillips, Nando Speranza, Des Styles and Bob Welsh have ensured that we have the creditors' view and not just a consultant's one.

This second edition is pretty true to the first book published in 2002, with some updating. I have added the final chapter on customer centric collections and scoring. Middleware system developments have meant that customer centric systems have become a real option for many businesses without the traditional hurdles of migrating from legacy systems or the cost usually associated with advanced collections systems.

Murray Bailey
May 2006

# CONTENTS

Foreword

### Part One: Management

Chapter 1 – The Importance and Role of Collections ...... 3

Chapter 2 – The Collections Process ...... 9

Chapter 3 – Attitudes Towards Debt Collection ...... 24

Chapter 4 – Motivation: The Deciding Factor ...... 33

Chapter 5 – Performance Measurement ...... 44

Chapter 6 – Capacity Planning ...... 57

Chapter 7 – Setting up a Collections Operation ...... 64

Chapter 8 – Auditing Collections ...... 72

Chapter 9 – Outsourcing ...... 80

### Part Two: Systems and Tools

Chapter 10 – Roll Rates and Probability of Write-off ...... 89

Chapter 11 – Cost Effectiveness ...... 96

Chapter 12 - Integrated Systems ...... 103

Chapter 13 – Using Diallers ...... 111

Chapter 14 – Problems and Problem Resolution ...... 119

Chapter 15 – Customer Centric Systems ...... 127

Chapter 16 – Open Systems and the Internet ...... 135

Part Three: Scoring and Strategies

Chapter 17 – Understanding Behavioural Scorecards ...... 145

Chapter 18 – Collections and Recovery Scoring ...... 156

Chapter 19 – Revenue Models ...... 166

Chapter 20 – Action Specific Models ...... 171

Chapter 21 – Why Scorecards Don't Work ...... 181

Chapter 22 – Basic Collections Strategies ...... 188

Chapter 23 – Leading Edge Collections Strategies ...... 195

Chapter 24 – Strategy Tracking and Efficiency ...... 204

Chapter 25 – Customer Centric Collections and Scoring ...... 211

Glossary of Terms ...... 217

About the Authors ...... 235

Index ...... 241

# FOREWORD

Increasing growth in credit markets worldwide, fuelled by increasing consumer spending and a cultural change in attitude to debt, is set to continue. With UK based Banks writing off £5.2 billion of consumer lending in 2005, residential mortgage loan arrears in Australia currently at their highest for 10 years, and US household debt including mortgages accelerating to $11 trillion last year, it is apparent that consumer debt is a global issue.

In this economic landscape, managing consumer debt and, in particular, the collection of monies owed becomes even more significant – reducing write-offs and revenue leakage while increasing the levels of revenue collected can make a measurable impact on an organisation's bottom line.

The Collections Manager plays a crucial role in the operation of any credit lending business. In many organisations the difference a successful collections department can make to bottom line profitability is often under-valued.

Businesses should recognise that Collections Managers have the power to add £millions to the bottom line, and therefore ensure that they have access to the best tools to manage the collections process with optimum efficiency.

Recognising the limitations of your current debt collection strategy and supporting your collections operation by investing in modern IT is the key to improving collections performance.

A modern collections system delivers measurable benefits including reduced bad debt write-off and lower levels of outstanding debt, increased cash flow and improved profitability as well as greater operating efficiency and strengthened customer relationships. These benefits mean that your return on investment can often be achieved in less than 12 months.

Investment in IT systems is just part of the ultimate solution. Deploying the full capabilities of the new system and enhancing business processes and working practices are also fundamental.

Research undertaken in 2005 shows that many collection departments are failing to utilise modern technology. Communication channels which customers are using, such as SMS and email, are under utilised, given the low cost associated with businesses using them. Today's delinquent customers, who force businesses to write off billions of pounds need to be tackled using today's technology.

Reading this book will give you an understanding of the vital role your collections operation plays in your business and how much it can contribute to your overall profitability and success. The contributions from experts contained within this book will equip you with the knowledge required to invest in appropriate resources and tools to ensure that your collections department is operating at optimum efficiency.

Brian Dewis
CEO, Talgentra Ltd
April 2006

# Part One

# Management

"The key challenge to introduce and maintain an effective performance measurement regime in collections and recoveries requires a clear understanding of the key drivers of performance."

Martyn Phillips, HBOS

# 1

## The Importance and Role of Collections
_by Murray Bailey_

**Why have a Collections function?**
If the business has priced for a level of risk, then why do we need a Collections function? Some start-ups actually ask this question thinking that the financial projections were assuming no additional resource. There is the apocryphal story of the business that removed collections activity. It was a small mortgage business and the management argued that the mortgage was the homeowner's highest priority debt. If they could not meet their obligations then something was seriously wrong and no amount of activity on behalf of the lender would remedy the situation. The business would take legal action at a set point following default and repossess the property. The recoveries would therefore cover the debt.

There were two fundamental issues with this logic. Firstly lenders have a responsibility to the debtors. They have an obligation to listen to problems and try and resolve them. The second issue was that the losses increased as a result of inaction.

For secured lending, delaying repossession usually means deterioration in the value of the goods. Vehicles depreciate, but houses also lose value due to neglect and, heaven forbid, deliberate damage.

So, does that mean that the simple strategy of wait then sue is appropriate for unsecured lending? Aside from the issue of it being 'unsecured' and therefore without a lien on property, there are two additional justifications for collections activity: cash flow and prevention.

Lending is about interest rate margins, integral to which is the speed at which the cash is repaid. If the money takes twice as long to be repaid, it costs the lender twice as much in funding costs. Poor cash flow management can wipe out the potential profits of an otherwise sound business.

**Profit and loss**
So, how much does a Collections operation save the business? The benefit of having a Collections operation is difficult to quantify and will depend on the credit product, the level of risk and the efficiency of the department. It is perhaps more sensible to look at the profit and loss (P&L) account and ask the question: "What is the trade-off between collections and write-offs?"

|  | £ millions | % |
|---|---|---|
| Interest Income | 34.4 | 18.1 |
| Cost of Funds | (12.1) | (6.4) |
| Net Interest Income | 22.3 | 11.7 |
|  |  |  |
| Operating Costs | (8.2) | (4.3) |
| Credit losses | (6.7) | (3.5) |
| Total Costs | (14.9) | (7.8) |
|  |  |  |
| Net Profit | 7.4 | 3.9 |

Table 1.1 Example P&L account

We will return to this question in the next section. In the meantime let us take the example of a credit card business. A summary of the P&L account is shown in table 1.1. The percentages in the table are each income and cost expressed as a percentage of the outstanding balances.

The first point to note from table 1.1 is the similarity between the credit losses and the profit. In other words, for every £ of profit there has been almost £1 of credit loss. So write-offs have a significant part to play in profitability. They are also highly sensitive, in particular to the economy.

'Credit losses' in the P&L account comprise of three elements: write-offs, recoveries and change in bad debt provision. Bad debt provisions (as defined in the Companies Act 1948) are "any amount written off by way of providing for depreciation in the value of assets". A general provision is made for accounts for which risk is recognised but that have yet to reach a defined point of write-off (a specific provision of 100%). The bad debt provision appears in the Balance Sheet to reflect the depreciated value of the assets (or debtor balances outstanding). The change in the provision is charged to the P&L account, in effect, accounting for expected write-offs. Recoveries are the monies received from written-off accounts. Its treatment as income will often affect the approach taken in managing and collecting the debt, as we will discuss in chapters 24 and 25.

Earlier, we asked the question: "What is the trade-off between collections and write-offs?" If we took the variable costs (people and materials) out of the credit card example in table 1.1, we would see a cost of collection of around £500,000.

In the drive for efficiency, senior management will often look to reduce this expense. However, compared with the write-offs, the variable collections costs are about 7.5%. Clearly the figures will vary from lender to lender, but this ratio is important. What it means is that less than a 4% improvement in credit losses would justify a 50% increase in collection costs.


**Getting the balance right**
There are three internal drivers of Collections results. These are: volumes, performance (or strategy) and people.
The volume of accounts will have many influences on results. Too few and economies of scale are not available. An example of this is discussed in chapter 10 on using powerdiallers to increase efficiency. The numbers of accounts entering collections must be forecast for capacity planning purposes. Similarly the volume of account in work queues must be estimated. Many a strategy has fallen foul of insufficiently allocated resource to work the cases.

Performance should be seen as the overall efficiency of write-off and collection costs rather than cash recovered. Soft debt is, by definition, easy to collect. It is a short-sighted Collections Manager who moves resource from later to earlier collections in order to get improvements in cash recovered. The volume of accounts rolling delinquent will be reduced and for a few months overall delinquency may improve. However, accounts becoming delinquent are now harder to collect and once there, the inadequate resource produces poorer results. The upshot is that losses increase.

People are the most important tool in collections. To perform well, they must be motivated by the right environment and rewards and should be both appropriately trained and skilled for the assigned responsibilities. Again, inadequate planning or deliberate under-resourcing will only result in poor performance in the long term.

These three factors are clearly inter-linked. Capacity planning depends on the volume of accounts and strategies employed. The success of a strategy depends on the allocation of people, at the appropriate time and with the right skills. Efficiency can only be gained by controlled strategy testing and evaluation, which in turn must be linked to collector performance and rewards.

With all the 'ducks lined up' the Collections Manager can still be caught out by external factors. The biggest of these is the economy. Recessions have a dramatic impact on collections performance. To make matters worse, the impact on customers, tends to be a leading indicator of the Government's measure of a downturn – two quarters of a decline in Gross Domestic Product (GDP). Cash recovered falls, more debtors enter hardship categories, volumes entering collections increase, roll rates deteriorate and of course write-offs increase.

Delinquency may double or even treble as a result of a recession. The typical senior management reaction to rising delinquency and losses is to implement radical changes. In these circumstances, fire-fighting is not the appropriate response. Nor is the rapid introduction of new and untested strategies. The reality is that it is too late. With the right culture and philosophy, the smarter Collections function will be forearmed and ready to minimise the impact of a downturn.

All the reasons for having a Collections department are magnified during a recession. More customers require counselling and debt advice, without which they would quickly progress to write-off. Cash flow is also critical at this time and the negotiation of an arrangement can prevent write-off, but, just as importantly, it will assist solvency.

Whilst write-off policies and provisions are accountancy rather than risk, they are none-the-less vital to the company's reported performance. Changes in policies or methodologies do not effect the underlying performance of the portfolio and can frustrate the modeller. Predicting write-off, or another element of delinquency, can be complicated when a company changes definitions. However, there are often good reasons for the changes. For example, during a recession it may be appropriate to change the minimum required instalment or the minimum acceptable settlement. Providing flexible solutions for debtors who want to work with the company to solve their problem, is a long term strategy. The solution for the modeller is to recreate the modelled history under the new policies and terms, thus reflecting the changed environment.

We began this chapter by arguing that Collections is vital. Unfortunately it is often seen as a necessary evil. Management may keep collections at arms length, depriving the operation of the support and board level responsibility that is often justified. This is a real issue for collections and Chapter 3 looks at this in relation to expenditure on systems.

# 2

## The Collections Process
_by Steve Holyoake and Nando Speranza

### Organisational Structure

The organisational structure in terms of centralised or branch based collections, is always a major talking point in any discussion about collections management.

A centralised collection function allows for more effective resource management. Fewer managerial resources are required to manage staff in one location than for a disparate workforce. Consistency is very important in collections management and this is significantly easier to achieve in a centralised environment. This affects collection policies, training, performance appraisal, collector measurement and reward structures.

A dedicated collections function ensures that there are adequate resources to manage the task effectively. Within a branch environment, individuals are often responsible for many other functions including sales, customer service, administration and branch management.

A major benefit of centralisation is having a dedicated resource, focused on a single goal. Focus generates knowledge, know how and expertise. There are no other distracting tasks to be performed. In a centralised environment there are sufficient volumes for specialisation of collectors – early delinquent accounts can be given to customer service oriented staff; another team can specialise in the harsher collections activity required for late stage delinquent accounts. Other specialisations can include policy group collections, fraud management, tracing, external agency management, legal aspects relating to recovery, first payment defaulters and so forth.

The volume-aspect also enables new software/technology to be brought to bear, providing proven techniques to enhance results:

- Sophisticated segmentation policies
- Scripting and policies
- Predictive diallers

De-centralised functions also have benefits: speed of response, the ability to develop deeper client relationships and a broader view of the client's personal situation. The greatest benefit of de-centralised collections is that the client can be invited to discuss their situation in person. It may also be possible to visit the customer if required. In this event, the branch staff have an existing relationship with the customer. Contact will also tend to be far more effective in eliciting payment promises.

However, in a de-centralised environment, the following statements are often true: Collections activities may not be the only task that staff are responsible for and therefore are often performed only when time allows; Management of the collection activity is done locally and therefore there is unlikely to be any great consistency and policies are likely to be very much specific to the particular office; Productivity is low because many of the technologies that could be used to improve it cannot be warranted for smaller offices.

## Specialisation

De-centralised operations allow for no specialisation. Collectors work all types of different accounts. This is known as a 'cradle to grave' system. Consideration of the arguments for 'specialisation' of collectors as opposed to working in a 'cradle to grave' environment is discussed below.

Certain tasks within a collections environment are highly specialised skills, for example, frauds, trace activities, legal actions. As such there is little debate that these tasks are more optimally performed by specialist rather than generalist collectors.

However, even if we exclude these tasks, the specialisation of collectors into teams dealing with specific levels of delinquent accounts has many advantages over working in a 'cradle to grave' manner.

The level of difficulty associated with collecting payments from accounts in each level of delinquency is different. It makes sense, therefore, that the skills and personality types required to be most effective will be different. Structuring the organisation into teams responsible for each different delinquency levels will allow the skills of individual collectors to be more optimally matched to the risk or quality of queues being worked, which will improve results.

Even within each level of delinquency, there are different levels of 'harshness' of action required. Collections strategies deal with this by segmenting accounts into different queues. The key, however, is that the message delivered to the debtors must be appropriate to the 'risk' of the queue. In order that this is carried out to optimum effect, better results can be achieved by allocating the best collectors within each specialist team to the harshest queues.

In conclusion, there is a clear case for a centralised collections function with fewer benefits associated with a de-centralised credit operation. The three major issues are control, focus and cost savings: With centralised management, control is improved as policies will be consistent throughout the entire organisation. This set-up also releases individual branches to focus and concentrate on the core competences like customer service. Centralisation also allows for cost savings through economies of scale and use of technology.

The remainder of this chapter looks at the centralised approach, although with the advent of internet home-working, it has the broader meaning of control by the centre rather than a single office.

**Stages and Actions**

A key business requirement for effective account management for all life cycle stages is the use of targeted and appropriate actions. Segmenting customer's accounts is a useful means of prioritising and 'targeting' appropriate actions. It provides the means for moving away from a 'one size fits all' approach. By grouping customers who 'look' the same or 'perform' in the same way, it is possible to match groups of customers to actions that are appropriate.

Within the collections process, there are many different types of action available. These actions should be altered by level of risk that the account represents. As a general principle, selecting the appropriate action for each segment of customers can be done by modifying three aspects:

- Type – e.g. call, letter, statement message
- Tone – e.g. harsh, medium or soft
- Timing – at which point during the cycle

It is typical for the collections process to be split into three or four functionally different areas. These areas are:

- **Over-limit not delinquent** (revolving product) - typically these accounts would receive a customer service call as a reminder to the customer of the status of their account
- **Early Stage delinquents** - here the focus will be on rehabilitating the customer
- **Late Stage delinquents** - the focus will be on recovering the balance or as much of it as possible. The customer is no longer wanted.
- **Policy groups** - these are for special circumstances – for example, deceased or fraudulent accounts, which require specialist actions and treatment.

This approach to structuring collections is an example of high-level segmentation. The next sections examine in more detail the processes that should be followed in each of these areas in turn.

### Over-limit not delinquent

This is a stage specific to revolving credit products where the balance is in excess of the credit limit. Although not overdue, the potential risk on these accounts warrants special treatment.

It is important in this area that any follow-up policies or procedures are consistent authorising policies. It would not be wise to allow overspend through authorisation policies and then take action on the account as a result of the spend.

It is common for this group, because of a low priority being assigned to this area within an organisation, to find 'one rule fits all' type policies based on the percentage over-limit or subjective decisions being made by individuals. However, today's high risk over-limit customers *will* become next month's high balance delinquent customers.

This can also be an area to watch out for fraudulent activity. This activity can be evidenced by 'runaway' spending, non-typical usage, or excessive usage after a new card has been issued.

Let us look at how segmentation would be used to build a better strategy for over-limit collections. The best way of illustrating or describing how to segment your portfolio is to use a decision tree diagram. Figure 2.1 illustrates a section of a decision tree in collections. Each segmented branch of the decision tree ends with a set of actions appropriate to the group described by the branch, in this case statement message, letter and work queue codes.

Segmentation is done on the basis of aspects of the account (shown on the left hand side of the diagram, in this case Ever Paid, Months on Books etc).  The values of each aspect are shown in the body of the diagram.

Starting at the left hand side, is a group of customers that have never paid ('Ever Paid' being equal to 'No'). These are further segmented into those slightly over-limit ('Percent Utilised' equal to 101 to 110) and those more seriously over-limit. Remember, these accounts are *not* delinquent, therefore they must be before their first payment due date. It is not good that they are over-limit at all in this early stage in the relationship. Therefore, it is appropriate, even for the slightly over-limit accounts, to get statement messages and letters with a medium harshness tone. They will not however be put in a work queue.

The more heavily over-limit accounts get a 'Hard' statement message and will be put straight into a work queue rather than sending a letter. The reasoning being that physical contact is likely to be more necessary on the more over-limit accounts than the mildly over-limit ones and one of the objectives is to maximise the collector resource.

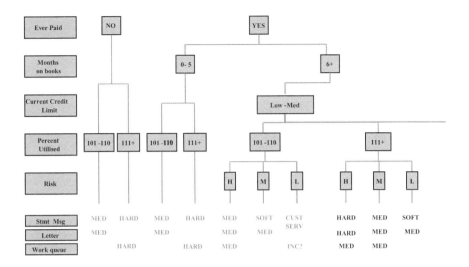

Figure 2.1 An over-limit, not delinquent decision tree

Accounts that have made some previous payments are first segmented by 'Months on Books' to split out accounts that are relatively new to the business. In this group there is a split based on 'Percent Utilised' and in fact similar actions are taken to the 'Never Paids', as these accounts are very similar.

For established accounts, two new aspects have been introduced to segment the accounts. Firstly, the 'Credit Limit', as it helps quantify the potential losses and will be used to tilt actions. Likewise a 'Risk' aspect is used as it is the strongest indicator of potential losses. The best tool for this is a behavioural score. If these are not available, proxies can still be used applying the same principles, for example:

- Time since last delinquent
- Max delinquency in past six months
- Months since max delinquency
- Number of times delinquent in past six months

So, the low to medium limit accounts that are mildly over-limit have been divided into three risk groups, high, medium and low.

Starting with the low risk group, these customers may only require a customer service-type statement message as a gentle reminder of their account status. In fact, increasing the credit limit might be considered. The medium risk group would face slightly more severe actions but this would most likely be a soft message in the statement and followed up by a slightly harsher letter. They would not however be put into work queues as the valuable resource is saved for the high risk group who also receive statement messages and letters with a moderately harsh tone.

Moving on to look at the accounts that are more heavily over-limit, a similar principle of tilting the actions would be applied. Thus, the actions given to the medium risk for the mildly over-limit group are now applied low risk, and the high-risk action moved to the medium risk group. The high-risk group that are more heavily over-limit, are treated with harsh messages and letters.

As can be seen, the type and tone of actions taken are altered for different groups, appropriate to their profiles. A similar process of tilting the actions would be done for accounts with high credit limits.

**Early Stage Delinquency**
The level of delinquency referred to here is typically one and two cycles delinquent. When dealing with early stages of delinquency, the objective is to rehabilitate the customer into a position where they can purchase again. The actions taken are therefore not going to be harsh. They are typically more customer service oriented – reminding customers of their obligations. Both telephone calls and letters are used however.

Segmentation is again a key to allocation of work and actions taken, being used to prioritise accounts for action. For example, within the first cycle, focus would initially be on the new First Payment Defaulters, then new over-limit accounts, and so on. The best tool for prioritisation is a behavioural score but as seen earlier proxies can be used.

Remember the objective of maximisation of resource effectiveness. Physical resources will be focused first on accounts that will not pay without a communication from the organisation. At the other end of the scale, the majority of the established, low risk accounts, will pay without communication being necessary, thus optimising the use of resource and reducing costs by not unnecessarily applying collection actions.

The objective of maintaining customer service, not chasing the lowest risk customers maintains customer service, as they probably simply forgot to make their payment on time.

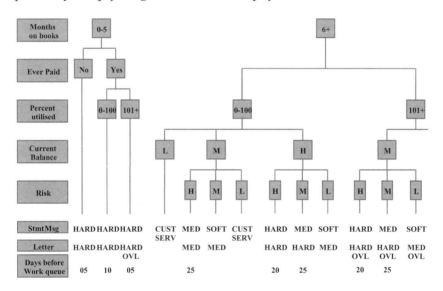

Figure 2.2 An Early stage collections decision tree

Now type, timing and tone of action is used to find the appropriate action for the different priorities. So let us look at a strategy for Cycle One accounts, designed along these principles using a decision tree diagram to illustrate (figure 2.2).

Firstly let us look at the 'New' accounts that have never paid. Clearly these are a very high-risk group of accounts. Appropriately they will receive 'Hard' statement messages and letters and will be placed in a work queue early on in the cycle.

'New' accounts that have paid previously are further segmented on the basis of their limit utilisation. Over-limit accounts are treated with the same priority as those that have never paid. They will receive an appropriately worded 'Hard' letter and Statement message. Those that are under limit will receive similarly harsh letters and messages but will not be put into work queues until later in the cycle. This is to give them the chance to correct their status before being called.

For the established accounts, segmentation on the basis of utilisation is used, to separate out over-limit accounts, as these represent higher risks. Those accounts that are within limit, typically have 'Current balance' used as a segmentor. This is to differentiate between low balances, where it may not be cost effective to consider a lot of action, and high balance accounts that represent high potential losses. Therefore, for the low balance accounts only a statement message is used, as this is the least expensive action. The message would be tailored to the circumstances and would most likely be a customer service type message. The medium balance accounts would be further segmented on the basis of a risk aspect, into high, medium and low groups.

In terms of risk breaks, the norm is for the high and low bands to cover about 25% of the total and therefore for the medium to be half of the group. These guidelines are used as it is vitally important to set up these breaks with an eye on the volumes of accounts that are going to fall down each leg, as it has a massive impact on the resource requirements.

As can be seen in the diagram, each of the actions is tilted, with the low risk group getting the softest approach and the high risk the harshest. The work queue has been set to day 25. This is in order that enough time is given to complete all the work from accounts put into queues earlier in the month, thereby utilising available resource optimally.

As can be seen, the high risk, high balance accounts drop into work queues before day 25. Again the tilting approach can be seen with actions getting softer/slower as the risk gets lower.

It can also be useful to compare similar risk groups across the medium and high balance groups: the same tilting principle can be seen. The same principles are used for over-limit accounts.

For collector calls, it is best practice to provide collectors with a script or guidelines of how to conduct the call. This helps to ensure that the correct content and tone of the conversation is carried out consistently across the resource and that it conforms to the strategy which you have worked out.

As seen, groups of accounts will be put into work queues at different times during the month as part of prioritising collections effort. Within each queue however, further sequencing or prioritisation will be needed to sort the accounts into an order list for the collectors. This is because, although the accounts have been assigned the same priority (hence being in the work queue), there can either be a particular circumstance or diarised action. A particular circumstance could be a broken promise which requires immediate action. The diarised action will require action on a specific date. There can still be further rank ordering within the group, for example based on score or balance.

## Late Stage Delinquency

Late Stage delinquency is typically defined as three or more cycles delinquent. The focus now shifts from rehabilitation of the customer to recovery of the debt. Even so, as in early stage collections, the allocation of work will be driven by segmentation of the portfolio, so that treatment can be appropriate whilst maximising the use of available resources.

The tools that get used when working in late stage collections will alter as the emphasis is now on recovery. Therefore, actions will be much harsher. Blocking of facilities is a recognition that, even if the account returns to a healthy position, the organisation no longer wishes to transact with the customer. Sometimes, it may be appropriate to offer the customer some kind of assistance by rescheduling the debt in some way. Adding the customers' details to 'negative files' operates as a cap on exposure by providing warning of poor performance. It can also be a catalyst for payments since other lenders may only lend once previous debts have been honoured. The transfer of accounts to external agencies is known to have a positive effect, simply based on the impact of the debt being administered by a different entity. Legal proceedings could be commenced if the situation warrants them.

As seen in the previous sections, many different aspects of an account can be used to ensure that appropriate action is taken. In the decision tree diagram in figure 2.3 best practice, in dealing with late stage delinquency, is examined. In terms of the actions to keep things simple, this illustration points out where it is best practice to use external agencies and where not to. When it is best to keep the accounts internal, a priority level has been assigned: 1 is high and 3 is low. This priority level would need to be 'fleshed out' with appropriate levels of statement messages, letters and work queue timings, using exactly the same principles of tilting based on risk which have already been covered in the previous sections.

Accounts that have never paid are undoubtedly very high risk and should almost certainly be handed over to an external agency for recovery or investigation. Accounts that have paid previously will typically be segmented on the basis of how long ago the last (acceptable) payment made was. Acceptable will be based on a percentage of an instalment or amount owing.

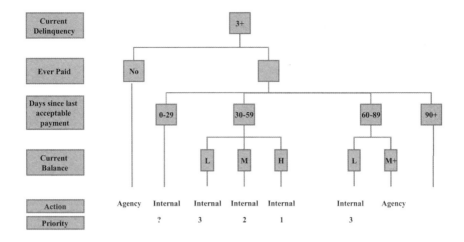

Figure 2.3 A Late stage collections decision tree

It is unlikely that you would want to hand over to an external agency those accounts that have made a payment in the last month.

There is a discussion point over the priority level of this group of accounts. One school of thought says they have just paid and therefore are lower risk, the other school says that the fact that they have just paid means they should be followed up strongly to ensure the payment stream continues to ensure stronger recovery.

The accounts that last paid in the previous month are further segmented on the basis of the balance owing and possibly a further level based on risk, although this is not shown here for simplicity. Again, it is unlikely that these accounts be handed over to external agencies based on the recency of last payment. The potential loss will drive the priority level, with the higher balances therefore being allocated the highest priority.

Continuing on the same basis, accounts which have not paid in the last two months and have medium or higher balances will now be handed over and only the low balance accounts will be kept back for another month. The priority assigned would be low on the basis of the potential size of the loss. All accounts that have not paid in the last three months would be handed over to an agency, irrespective of the size of the balance.

Some delinquent debtors do not react until they receive communication from a separate legal entity. Therefore, it can be good practice to establish an internal agency operating under a different identity. This creates the perception of an escalation of seriousness and treatment and may have significant cost benefits.

One of the main objectives of any collections environment must be to optimise the cost-income ratios. It is vital therefore that there is a good understanding of when it is not cost effective for collections to be pursued internally. Internal departments are a fixed cost regardless of success in recovery. External agencies are normally only paid for success.

## Policy groups

'Policy groups' covers a whole list of special circumstances that require special treatment. Some of these areas will have to be dealt with on an account by account basis as it difficult to devise specific policy rules to deal with the various circumstances – each account has to be dealt with on its merits. However, there may still be policies applied to each set, for example based on the size of the potential losses, different levels of scrutiny may be appropriate.

The list below shows most of the groups of accounts where it is typical to find special policy rules applied.

- Lost/Stolen
- Disputed
- Unpaid debit order
- Insurance claim
- Change in personal circumstances

- Fraud
- Skip tracing
- Deceased
- Bankrupt

We have discussed the breakdown of the Collections function into very different areas. Even though the focus for each area is quite distinct, and should be resourced with specialists each receiving appropriate training for their area, they share a common goal of minimising bad debt losses, maximising collector effectiveness and the maintenance of good customer service.

# 3

# Attitudes Towards Debt Collection
*by Rae Miller*

## Prosperity

*If you want one year of prosperity, grow seeds,*
*If you want ten years of prosperity, grow trees,*
*If you want one hundred years of prosperity, grow people*
Chinese proverb

It is true to say that in many organisations, collections management is treated like a poor relation, and as a function its contribution (and therefore that of its team members) is grossly undervalued. It is probably also fair to say that very few organisations use the collections function as a primary source of improvement initiatives. Added to this, many newly established organisations treat collections as an after thought rather than an essential part of their business plan.

In this chapter, we look at the lot of the Collections Manager and his staff and the importance of the collections function in identifying opportunities and leading change in the organisation. We also look at best practices and technological advances that make change possible and the barriers to change that Collections departments may face.

Recent research looked at the attitudes towards debt collection and systems. The research questioned 120 organisations involved in consumer collections, of which 37% were in the finance sector, with the balance coming from the utilities and local authorities.

The research revealed that while bad debts are often a high profile and sensitive issue, the debt collection process itself is for the most part an in-house, low profile activity. This is evidenced by the responsibility of the person in charge of the function, the lack of board level representation, the processes they use and the age of the systems used to help the activity.

The research also found that there is generally a limited pro-active management of the debt collection process. Many of the respondents claim to be monitoring costs and managing the activity, but there is strong evidence to the contrary. The key findings were that: 40% of respondents do not know the total amount of debt outstanding within their departments; 62% of companies did not know the cost of their debt collection activities, and; 64% of companies did not know the departmental cost of the activity, even though for the most part it is centralised.

**Best practice in debt collection**

The issue facing many collections professionals is how to make companies appreciate that an investment in collections management adds real bottom line value. It is not enough to state the obvious that, the lower the bad debt and the quicker cash is collected, the better the bottom line performance. Could the Collections Manager offer more and be hailed as the hero or heroine of the organisation?

One thing is certain, weaknesses and failings of processes within an organisation usually manifest themselves as collections issues. For example: I've been charged for a service I haven't received; You haven't sent me the direct debit mandate I requested; I haven't had the bill; I cancelled the service months ago; You've cashed my cheque, how dare you chase for payment; The bill doesn't add up.

The list is endless. The fact is that, aside from those cases where there is genuine lack of ability to pay, every excuse is either a variation on 'the cheque is in the post' or demonstrates a real failing on the part of the business. The Collections Manager therefore has the greatest exposure to the weaknesses in a company's processes. He is also best placed to recognise opportunities to improve efficiencies within the organisation.

So, let us assume that the Collections Manager can exploit this opportunity to improve processes – how will this impact on other areas of the business?

Process improvements that are suggested by the Collections Manager and taken on board by the organisation can mean that the bill is more likely to be received by the right customer in the right format, at the right time. Those that can pay, will pay. Cash flow will improve; administration costs will decrease, so margins will improve. And, ultimately, the bottom line is enhanced.

Improved processes can also have a positive effect on the company's marketing strategy. An overall reduction in costs may provide the flexibility to reduce prices, an essential part of the marketing mix. This could be key to expanding sales or as a defensive strategy in a competitive marketplace. By increasing sales and maintaining margin, the bottom line is again improved.

Ultimately, an improvement in processes will have a positive effect on customer satisfaction. Every contact a customer has with an organisation is important and removing some of the negative customer experiences will undoubtedly improve the relationship with the customer base. With increased competition in areas such as telecommunications, 'churn rates' are high. Improved customer service will reduce this rate of customers leaving.

In order to influence an organisation and to improve collections processes, it would be in the interest of the Collections Manager to investigate collections management best practices adopted by other organisations. It is important to understand that debt collection performance is not just a factor of a customer's willingness to pay. Collections Managers must put themselves in control and start to understand and adopt the approaches that have worked well for other organisations.

### Bill; bill quickly; bill accurately

Best practice dictates that customers billing requirements are taken seriously. Make it easy for customers to pay – ask them at the point of setting up the account which payment method will suit them best. Listen to the customer requirements, be honest about whether you can meet their requirements and agree a payment method.

Timely billing will also go some way towards taking control of collections. Best practice suggests that bills should be raised within 24 hours of the goods or services having been received.

It goes without saying that in order to bill accurately, you need to have all the relevant customer information in place prior to your billing run. It is a fact that inaccurate bills are rarely paid and in the event of non-payment, it is important to establish whether it is due to a billing inaccuracy or an issue relating to the customer's ability to pay.

### Can't pay or won't pay?

Difficulties often arise when trying to identify whether a customer cannot or will not pay. Collections Managers must ensure that any action taken to collect a debt is the result of an informed decision and not simply 'gut feel'. Cynics might choose to believe that customers find any excuse for not paying, but the reality is that most customers want to pay.

If the customer genuinely cannot pay, it is in the interest of the Collections Manager to discover this fact quickly. Appropriate action can then be taken. It may be better to support the customer, agree a payment plan and ultimately collect the debt rather than alienate the customer and spend time and money pursuing the debt.

Many customers are encouraged to pay their bills by direct debit, and it is worth establishing early if this is a payment method that the customer is happy with.

**Not all customers are the same**
It sounds obvious, but all customers are different and one approach to debt collection will not fit all customer types. Most organisations will adopt collection strategies to manage accounts with the same characteristics in the same way.

The most successful Collections departments will identify different types of debtors and deal with them accordingly. For example, a customer who has failed to make the first payment, may have done so because he has not received the relevant paperwork to make the payment. Similarly, a customer who has failed to make a last payment, may have done so because his direct debit cancellation has been a little premature. These are common reasons for non-payment and require different treatment from a customer who repeatedly falls into arrears. Such customers would be dealt with quickly, and the team would adopt a much tougher approach in order to collect the debt, possibly agreeing and closely monitoring a payment plan.

**Knowing the make up of the arrears book**
Many Collections teams are measured on the number of accounts they have in arrears. A best practice approach would be to fully understand the types of debtors making up the arrears book. A Collections department with 5,000 accounts in arrears might find

that a large proportion of the debt belongs to customers who have possibly died, or whose payments are made by the DSS. By examining the debtor profiles in the arrears book, the Collections Manager will be in a better position to concentrate on the collectable debt.

## Bad debt provision

An important part of a Collections Managers role should be to accurately forecast bad debt provision. Current technologies use historical data on debt, to forecast future bad debt provision.

## Changing the organisational structure

The approach to managing customer accounts will influence how you choose to structure the collections department. There are several ways to organise resources and no one way is always right. Some departments choose to split their teams horizontally, vertically or a mixture of the two. A horizontally split team would group staff managing similar tasks together, such as account reconciliation, copy invoice production, cash allocation or collection calling. Team members become specialists within one area, but morale may suffer as a result of not seeing the whole process through. A vertical approach ensures that a dedicated team handles every element of the customer relationship. This may be expensive to support, but the benefit of building a strong customer relationship should also be considered.

## Cross functional responsibility

The responsibility for debt collection should not rest exclusively with the Collections department. All business functions within an organisation can impact on a customer's willingness to pay. Collections Managers often become frustrated at not meeting their collections targets as a result of other people in the organisation failing to deliver. Some companies have therefore introduced collections related goals for their Sales teams. An example of this is a company who incentivised the Sales force to convert existing customers onto direct debit payment. The team achieved a conversion rate of 30 per cent in the first month, leading to cash flow improvements and the ability to project cash receipts more accurately. There is also the additional benefit of feedback to the Sales team to ensure that future campaigns are better targeted.

## Debt recovery guidelines

It is an essential requirement of best practice, that an organisation's debt recovery guidelines are well documented and regularly updated as circumstances change.

Many organisations now recognise the need to constantly review and adapt their existing range of debt recovery procedures in order to ensure that they are maximising their ability to collect debt from their customers. The Water Industry in the UK is a typical example. From 1999 it became illegal for any water company in the UK to disconnect for non-payment.

Each water company will have revised its strategy for debt collection since the 1999 ban on disconnections. Companies report that many innovative methods of collection are effective only until customers are used to them. A flexible approach can therefore be the key to making contact and re-establishing payment habits.

## Barriers to improving collections processes

Research has indicated that Collections departments see one main barrier to improving the efficiency of their collections processes. Inefficient legacy IT systems appear to be the most commonly identified barrier that Collections Managers face. Problems include; poor systems prevent departments from setting and meeting collections targets – this has a direct impact on cash collection; systems are so slow that extra resources are required to collect debt and inefficient IT systems add to the workload in the department.

The main business/IT issues being faced by Collections departments is summarised in table 3.1. Of 120 respondents, 75 were local authority or utilities and 45 from the finance industry. Figures in the table are percentages.

| Business/IT Issue | Total | Local Authority | Finance |
|---|---|---|---|
| *Base* | *120* | *75* | *45* |
| Inefficient IT System | 27 | 28 | 21 |
| Continued Long Term Debts | 20 | 18 | 19 |
| Converting to a New IT Solution | 6 | 5 | 7 |
| Other | 15 | 15 | 6 |
| None | 44 | 41 | 49 |

Table 3.1 Business issues by sector

There was also a concern amongst respondents that more accounts will be in arrears in the next two years, reflecting increased workloads for the companies who are perhaps already stretching their limited IT systems. Only a quarter of managers expected to be able to increase staff levels, even though staff are already over-stretched.

Another barrier to change highlighted in the research is that, although most managers saw benefits in improving their computer systems, few had the authority to make purchase decisions. Almost 60% of respondents responsible for bad debt, have no board level representation, whereas the authority for capital expenditure lay with the board in 80% of cases.

Whatever collection strategy an organisation chooses to adopt, it makes sense to optimise the use of available technology. As part of the strategy to improve the profile of the Collections department, it is worth taking a look at the available technologies to help manage the collections process. In today's competitive marketplace, it is increasingly important to select a collections system that allows you to meet business, operations and IT expectations.

Collections departments have come a long way since Shylock demanded his pound of flesh and it may be some time still before the Collections Manager takes his place on the board. However, attitudes are starting to change towards the role of the Collections Manager. They are becoming viewed as skilled professionals who have a broad range of skills and tools, from power diallers to behavioural scoring strategies; from customer account management to champion/challenger functionality and analysis.

The Chinese proverb is undoubtedly true. However, those people also need the tools and the authority to make the difference.

# 4

## Motivation: The Deciding Factor
_by Donna Guest

**Foundation**

Take an assortment of seeds, put them in a sealed box and leave them under the stairs. What happens? Nothing. The seeds just sit there, minding their own business and not changing one little bit.

Now take that same assortment of seeds, plant them in a nutritious soil, give them plenty of water and bathe them in rich, warming sunlight. Now what happens? The seeds react to their stimuli and start to grow, reaching out towards what they want: more sunlight.

No, this is not a chapter on horticulture that has sneaked in unnoticed by the editor, it is an illustration of how providing the right stimulus can revolutionise behaviour. In the case of seeds a firm foundation in soil and water plus direct sunlight stimulates a positive reaction.

To make people react you need to find what stimulates them and then provide that stimulus in a controlled and measured fashion to improve their performance and stimulate personal and corporate growth. What follows is an exploration of how this principle can be applied to credit management teams.

### Turning cost into income

Credit management is a large, technically challenging, potentially arduous but vitally important process. The simple truth is, without effective credit management, all the sales in the world will not make your company successful – it is money in the bank that counts.

But this is not news. Most companies recognise the key role of credit management and devote serious budgets to the process. The mistake that all too many organisations make is that the credit control system is treated too much like a production line. By investing that little bit extra time and money in your credit management system you can change it from just another 'thing that you just have to have' into a source of increased profitability and clear competitive advantage. The area to focus on is the human element.

If you treat people like machines they behave like machines, only ever producing what they are required to, sometimes less. If, on the other hand, you treat people like people, by stimulating, motivating and rewarding them, you get much, much more. If you give people a reason to perform above and beyond the call of duty then that is what they will do. But much more, they become a source of new ideas and new ideas are where your company will find competitive advantage.

### Motivational map

The first step is to know your team. Some you may know, some you may not. It is important that you get an understanding or 'motivational map' of what their ambitions and fears are. By understanding what drives them, you can target your motivational strategy to appeal to your team and so produce the best results.

Involve your people in drawing your motivational map. Be up front about your programme. Explain what your objectives are; maximising profitability. If your credit management team see themselves as a source of profit, rather than trying to minimise loss, it will give morale a boost.

Ask your team what they would like. By giving people a stake in the creation of an incentive scheme you get them to take ownership of it, so creating greater participation and commitment once a particular programme begins.

However you arrive at it, you need to build a motivational map of your team, in as great a level of detail as time and team size will permit. It is this motivational map that will show you the route to take with your incentive programme.

The map will not be perfect first time, you need to keep it constantly updated and corrected. As you introduce each new incentive scheme you should carefully monitor its success; it is only by testing an incentive that you will really find out if it works for your team. The only way to find a winning formula is to test, test, test.

Once you have tested a variety of incentives remember the ones that work, amend the ones that do not, then test again. In time you will build up a tool box of incentives that you know will work and work well.

## Money
Money is a powerful motivator for two reasons, both deeply embedded in human nature. First, people want money, but we already know that. Second, money is measured by numbers and numbers are how the human mind understands the world.

Numbers are the fundamental language of comparison: distance, weight, space, time and crucially, they measure levels of success. Numbers are how we decide who has won and who has lost.

People cannot help but compare themselves to each other. This can be used to nurture a sense of friendly rivalry, between individuals within a unit and between units in the wider team.

Set fundamental targets for performance and reward them with clearly defined amounts of money. These are absolutes – the rules of a particular incentive. But also make sure that the best performing individuals and units are recognised.

Run a league table and keep it updated as regularly as possible. Make it a talking point so that it stays close to the front of everyone's mind. If you only update a leaderboard every Friday afternoon then few people will think about it regularly. Update it twice a day and your team will be thinking about it all the time, so making the incentive really *work*.

The kudos of being top individual or top unit will enhance the basic motivation of extra earnings derived from hitting specific levels and targets.

This is where the principal of testing can start to work. Do you achieve higher performance by just comparing_individuals? Is it best just to compare units with each other? Do you compare units and individuals? And what about reward? Is the cachet of being top performer enough to motivate, or do you get even higher performance by giving a specific financial bonus to the top unit / individual at the end of each day / week / month?

As you can see, the possible combinations are almost endless, but it really is worth testing different formulae to see which produce the best results.

However you structure the rewards for success, one thing to bear in mind is that the objective is to stimulate maximum success and never to inhibit anyone's effort or progress. In other words, there should never be a ceiling on the level of reward offered as an incentive. As soon as you put a ceiling on targets that ceiling will never be exceeded, because the motivation to try harder and go further simply is not there.

## Take aim

Some overdue accounts are easier to recover than others. Recovering a debt that is one month overdue is an awful lot more straightforward than recovering a debt that is one *year* overdue.

Depending on your accounting provision, the older debt may already have been written off completely, so any funds that your team can recover will be going straight back onto the bottom line.

The beauty of constructing an incentive scheme is that you can target these heavily overdue debts by rewarding them specifically.

Older debt is just one example. Targeting incentives can be used to improve results of any hot spot you may want to focus on: direct debit penetration, recovering accounts or reinforcing hold date management – whatever.

## Better late than never

When defining your incentive and reward structure care should be taken not to constrain your people into having to recover funds in one particular way. One of the key traits you are trying to encourage with an incentive scheme is to get your people thinking, not just grafting. That means they should have the freedom to negotiate with customers, not just stick rigidly to a formulaic script.

The trend in the industry is for incentive schemes to reward the negotiation of promises from customers to start paying through instalments, providing these commitments are kept for a certain period (typically three to six months).

If your team are going for broke and pushing for an 'everything now or not at all' because that is the only way they will hit their targets, then you are throwing away a potentially large chunk of money. Your incentive scheme should accommodate the long-term view.

## Keep it simple

You need to make your incentive scheme as simple as possible. Simple propositions are easy to understand and capture the imagination more readily than complex ones.

If people have a clear and simple understanding of what their objective is, they can direct all their energies towards reaching that target. If, on the other hand, they have a complex mixture of targets to hit, then the message is diluted and your team might get distracted trying to work out what they should be looking to do, rather than getting on and achieving it.

But there is another good reason to keep things simple: trust. If you are introducing a new incentive scheme (especially if it is to do with money) then you may encounter a certain amount of scepticism and reserve. If that new scheme is intricate and convoluted then you might get a certain feeling of 'management trying to pull a fast one'. If, on the other hand, your incentives are simple and transparent, then your team will see what is in it for them, what is in it for you and get into the spirit much more readily.

### Don't let the dust settle

Another facet of human nature you must address is the tendency to 'get comfortable'.

Any incentive scheme you offer your staff must be recognised as something extra in recognition of extra effort and extra achievement and never just part of the basic package. No one should feel that a bonus is part of their due.

Your incentive scheme should be a constant reminder of the commercial reality that employees of a large organisation can sometimes loose sight of: get results and you make money, do not get results and you do not get money.

To this end, you should give incentives a deadline. If people know that there is a set period of time in which they can take advantage of an offer, they go for it while they can, so improving productivity.

### Playing the system

Bear in mind, when you are formulating your rewards structure, that you are encouraging your people to think laterally, act on their own initiative and come up with inventive solutions to credit management problems. Take care that you do not open a Pandora's Box.

People, being people, might be a little *too* inventive and stick to the letter, if not the spirit of your incentive scheme. In other words, watch out for anyone playing the system. The targeting of older debt may be particularly vulnerable to this problem. A cynical mind may let a debt ripen with age in order to reap a higher bonus later, for example. Adapt your structures to guard against this possibility.

Making your incentives as simple and straightforward as possible should help to minimise this problem, as will a clear statement of the rules for the reward structure. It goes without saying that your systems will already have proof and verification mechanisms built-in.

With the best laid plans in the world you are still going to be vulnerable to a little 'gamesmanship' on the part of some members of the team – there are many more brains thinking about how the incentive will work in practice than yours, you are out-numbered.

If you do encounter problems, bring the particular promotion to a logical, but not hurried, conclusion and put the experience down as part of your never ending education. It bears repetition: test, test, test.

## Professional development

It is not just money that motivates people, there are many other levers you can use to stimulate, recognise and reward high performance levels. While people will always respond well to financial reward, they need to feel that they are growing and developing as individuals and that they are not just 'doing a job' but pursuing a *career*.

### Training

The first step towards building professional self-esteem is training. Not only does it equip people with the skills they need to do their job better, it sends a range of valuable messages. It tells people that they are valued by the company and that they are considered to be worth the investment of time and money. It also indicates that the job they are being trained for requires skill and not just anyone can do it, thereby raising the role's perceived value within the wider context of the company. Finally, it adds to people's self-value – having training under your belt is a clear example of personal growth and development.

The next logical step beyond training is qualification. The setting and passing of goals in the form of exams or some other academic standards raises the perceived value of the individual even further. What is more, it gives out very clear signals: any member of staff prepared to make the commitment and invest the effort, preparing themselves to attain a qualification standard, obviously takes what they are doing seriously.

Recognise their effort. Try to help them – pay for training and exams, help them find the time to study and make their success as high profile as possible within the company.

Training and qualification will help you spot those within your team who have ambition, talent and, most important, commitment. Cherry-pick the best of them and encourage them to work towards the next level: full professional recognition.

Anyone prepared to take on the responsibility and commitment of working towards a professional qualification is clearly someone you need to hang onto. Promote them. Look after them. Make sure everyone in the team understands their success and use that success as an example of what is available to everyone within the company. If people believe that they have a future within the firm then they will work harder to succeed.

*Awards*

Awards are the most visible way to motivate and encourage your staff. It is an unambiguous vote of support for those that have done conspicuously well and acts as a lift for the whole team. It is not just a jolly, it makes business sense. The motivational factors of awards work at several stages. Firstly, actually making the entries and the company going to the trouble of funding them is a vote of confidence. Going back over past success is a reminder of what people are capable of. Secondly, when nominations are announced it gives a lift to everyone on the shortlist.

Then the awards themselves: It is a great team bonding exercise to put on evening attire and go to a large industry event, mix with the competition, swap stories and generally let your hair down. The morale boost of actually winning goes without saying.

At every stage from start to finish, the awards process should be publicised within the company and any success should be pushed externally as well, getting maximum benefit from the exercise.

A fringe benefit of winning awards is that your company is recognised very publicly as valuing and encouraging its people, which makes recruitment of good people that bit easier.

*Nice place to work*
With all this effort in motivating your team you should not overlook the basics: giving your people a pleasant working environment. It is difficult to feel upbeat and go that extra mile if your surroundings are getting you down.

There is no need to go over the top, you do not need to give everyone an executive leather chair, just make sure your team's environment is not shabby, overcrowded or stuffy.

Make sure people have the right tools for the task. Once again, you do not need to replace the PCs every six months, just make sure that the equipment you are asking people to work with is up to the job and reasonably close to current developments, so that it does not present any obstacles to getting the job done.

Fail to address these simple, but important points and you create de-motivating factors that inhibit performance and need extra motivation to overcome.

**It doesn't cost a penny**
Incentives that motivate and encourage results that directly impact the bottom line are cost effective. The most obvious measure of this is in a direct bonus scheme for recovered debt. The

financial rewards you give to your team are self-funding because they are bringing in *extra* money above the costs of the bonuses.

This self-funding argument can also be extended to other elements in the motivational mix – training, qualification, awards and environment etc. Although the relationship is less cut and dried, anything that improves productivity increases income, so justifying the expenditure.

Credit and Collections Management is increasingly recognised as a highly skilled job. Understanding the complex factors affecting success and motivation are difficult, which is probably why increasing numbers of companies are outsourcing it to specialists.

Investing in motivating your people makes hard business sense. Quite simply, it does not cost money, it *makes* money. Skilled staff are your biggest asset and best tool in the collection and recovery of debt.

# 5

# Performance Measurement
_by Martyn Phillips_

## Layers

A traditional army marches on its stomach. A collections and recovery army marches on its performance feedback.

Performance measurement feedback needs to play to a range of audiences. Before looking at the measures, we should first understand the layers.

_Organisation layer_ – Driving high level strategic decision making such as agreement to invest in the credit management functions. Whilst collections and recovery people are business people first and foremost, there is a heavy reliance upon technology to maximise efficiency, particularly in larger scale operations. It is not untypical for investment in these key functions to tail off during the more benign periods of the business cycle, leading to 'knee jerk' action when trading conditions take a turn for the worse. An optimal performance measurement system will provide regular feedback to the top of an organisation to ensure that investment of people and technology in the collections and recovery functions keeps pace with the business cycle.

*Departmental layer* – Driving local strategic/tactical operational decision-making such as prioritisation of projects within the collections and recovery departments. Providing evidence of the key trends affecting the business, such as seasonality.

*Operational layer* – Driving short-term tactical resource decisions. Providing the basis for competitive benchmarking of operational team performance both internally and externally. Might support team-based incentives and tactical resource of calling campaigns.

*Individual layer* – Providing a framework for agent and line manager/coach to agree where the agent is performing well and areas that need work. Can also form the basis of competitive benchmarking of individual agents. Applications of individual performance data include recognition, personal development planning and remedial performance management. For example, an agent might be highly productive (raw promise to pay volume) and appear effective (kept promise rate) but have a low average kept promise value. This scenario might indicate weak negotiation skills and lead to appropriate training or coaching effort.

## Key Drivers

The challenge to introduce and maintain an effective performance measurement regime in collections and recovery requires a clear understanding of the key drivers of performance. This area of the business is extraordinarily data rich. The skill is in converting the data into information that can drive value-added action that is consistent with the goals of the organisation.

Let us consider some of the wealth of resources at the disposal of management:

- Organisation strategy
- Organisation business plans
- Industry/sector economic information

- Internal (say call centre) and external benchmark information
- Budget and cost information from finance
- Inventory information from account host, collection and risk management systems
- Effort and contact information from collection, outbound calling and inbound call systems
- Employee hours, work and attendance patterns from the human resources or staff scheduling systems

So, it is really complicated then? Well, not necessarily.

A rating agency (Standard and Poor for example) was visiting the Collections department of a scale lender in the UK. A question was posed to the Senior Collections Manager: "What is your collection strategy?" The Collections Manager, a man of considerable experience in the function replied: "Well, we 'phone them or we don't". This really happened and demonstrated that the panoply of tools, technology and people that is collections and recovery can quite easily be distilled into what really matters.

The trick in establishing an effective performance measurement regime in collections and recovery is to report on what really matters. The ideal is that information reported to each layer cascades both up and down to provide a continuous link between the goals of the organisation and the contribution of the collection or recovery agent.

The remainder of this chapter will focus on the key foundation layer of the performance measurement system, namely agent contribution.

## Collections vs. Recovery
Consideration should be given to differentiation of these two functions when measuring performance. Whilst the data components will have much in common, there is likely to be a

difference in emphasis. Typically, collections are about resolving a problem with a view to continuing the relationship with the customer. In recoveries however, whilst standards of customer care will be maintained, the relationship is typically terminated with the customer and the focus is on cost effectively minimising exposure to net loss.

## Ground rules

Briefly, before we look at some specific performance measurement options, it is worth reminding ourselves of a well-worn acronym that applies equally in collections and recovery as in other business areas.

Performance measures should be **SMART**:

- **S**pecific
- **M**easurable
- **A**chievable
- **R**ealistic
- **T**ime scaled

Thus a collector objective of 50 promises to pay per hour would be specific, measurable and time scaled, but might not be realistic or achievable.

## Assumptions

When considering performance measurement options in collections and recovery the following business imperatives are assumed:

*Bad debt provision and write-off* – It is assumed that the collection and recovery functions are key stakeholders in the delivery of an organisation's bad debt provision and write off plans.

*Operational costs* – It is assumed that the collection and recovery functions are constrained by budgets and expected to deliver value for money.

## Performance measurement in collections

Collections embraces delinquent accounts from the point that they have not paid, to the point of hand over to recovery. Measures should be in place to encourage high levels of productivity with the emphasis on thoroughness and quality escalating as the degree of delinquency escalates. Clearly you do not want to be paying for a full blown financial examination of your one payment down (cycle 1) customers if experience shows that 8 or 9 out of 10 of them will pay up from a light touch telephone call.

### Promise to pay per hour

Promise to pay per hour (PPH), is a very common performance measure in collections. On its own it is a productivity measure. It will typically be tracked and viewed alongside contact efficiency measures and promise quality tracking.

Components of this metric are agent time logged on and the number of negotiations concluded with a promise to pay during that time.

In table 5.1 we examine the impact of a light touch standard of say 12 promises per hour on cycle 1 versus a standard of say 6, implying a more in depth examination of the customer's circumstances on each call, on collection costs.

So, from a production perspective it is clear to see how easy it is to double collection costs.

There is of course a second view that needs to be taken. What is the impact of the increased collection intensity at six PPH on the bad debt provision charge? What if the cure rate is increased from 80% to 90%?

| PPH standard | Account Volume | Agent hours required | Agents required | Cost per agent | Total cost of agents |
|---|---|---|---|---|---|
| 12 | 9600 | 800 | 6.2 | 15000 | £92,308 |
| 6 | 9600 | 1600 | 12.3 | 15000 | £184,615 |

Note - One full time equivalent (FTE) provides 130 hours per month calculated as 37.5 hours per week*52/12, factored to 80% to account for holiday and sickness absence

Table 5.1  The impact of variable PPH standards on costs

| PPH standard | Account Volume | Average balance | Inventory Value | Cure rate | Roll rate | Prov$^n$ Rate | Provision charge |
|---|---|---|---|---|---|---|---|
| 12 | 9600 | £1,000 | £9,600,000 | 80% | 20% | 10% | £192,000 |
| 6 | 9600 | £1,000 | £9,600,000 | 90% | 10% | 10% | £96,000 |

Table 5.2 The impact of variable PPH standards on provision costs

In table 5.2 it is assumed that accounts that are not cured attract a provision against bad debt of 10% of the balance outstanding.

The position is not so clear now. In this example the additional cost of the more intensive collection standard (£92,308) is more than offset by a reduction in the bad debt provision charge (£96,000). The opportunity to experiment with different productivity standards and measure the net outcome is however clear. It is further worth mentioning that 'best practise' indicates that standards should vary as accounts progress through the stages of delinquency to reflect the increasing depth of attention required to cure an account.

Promise per hour is a well-established measure of productivity in collections. As we have seen it needs to be viewed alongside other measures to be sure that optimum business performance is achieved.

*Contact efficiency*

Contact efficiency should be considered at the department and individual level. A meaningful measure of contact efficiency from outbound collection calling campaigns is the 'right party contact rate'. This metric is made up of the number of successful customer contacts expressed as a proportion of the number of outbound calls placed. Collection operations benefiting from the use of a power dialler are able to dispose of the majority of dead call effort, such as no answers and engaged tones, without wasting a collection agent's valuable time. Where contact is made and the call is passed to an agent a wrap up code is typically used at the end of the call to indicate whether the contact was made with the target customer rather than a third party.

Over time collections management learn the best times to call various groups of customers leading to smart scheduling of campaigns and increased efficiency.

The contact efficiency of individual collection agents is monitored by measuring their availability to take calls. Data components include 'ready time', 'talk time' and typing or 'wrap up time'. When average talk time is tracked it can give an insight into an agent's call control capability when viewed alongside others. Similarly a higher than average typing or wrap up performance can indicate a training need for the valuable 'talk and type' skill.

*Promise kept rates*

It is all very well making contact with an overdue customer and negotiating an agreement to pay, but do the customers keep to their side of the bargain?

The elements of a promise to pay are an agreed sum to be paid and an agreed date for it to be paid by. It is quite common for collection businesses to build tolerances around this measure. For example, allowance might be made for the payment arriving a couple of days either side of the agreed date. Alternatively, a sum received greater than or equal to 95% of the recorded promise value might be accepted as a 'kept' promise.

There are various ways of tracking kept promise rates but probably the most reliable is to measure them at the point of maturity. For a typical measurement period of a calendar month an agent might have 300 promises reach maturity. If 200 pay on time and within tolerance the promise kept rate for the period is 200 divided by 300, which is 66%. As with most collection performance measures, kept promise rates should not be viewed in isolation. Here is one way of thinking about kept promise rates:

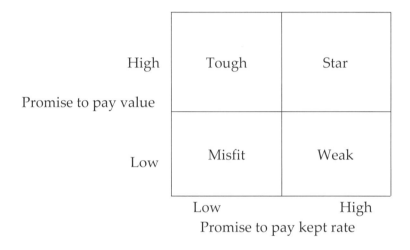

Figure 5.3 The promise to pay model

The Boston Matrix in figure 5.3 is one way of looking at kept promise performance to drive personal development effort. An agent with a high kept rate but a low average kept promise value falls in the 'weak' quadrant. Training for an agent here would be around negotiation with the aim of teaching him or her to drive harder bargains. Over time, managers would expect to see collector kept promise performance trending toward the top right hand quadrant of the model.

*Cost per £ 1 collected*

This measure is calculated by apportioning collections operating costs to money collected. The trend in the cost per £1 collected over time provides a valuable insight into the operational efficiency of a collections department. It may also provide feedback on the 'collectability' of debt being managed. This is a good example of a metric that can be tracked at the individual agent level and rolled up to give organisation level feedback against the key performance indicator of cost efficiency.

Table 5.4 is based on realistic assumptions of what might be seen in a retail financial services collection environment and clearly demonstrates how the cost of collecting £1 escalates as the level of delinquency increases.

| Cycle | Account volume | Agent hours | £'s collected | Apport-Ioned costs | PPH | Promise kept rate | Average value paid | Cost per £1 collected |
|---|---|---|---|---|---|---|---|---|
| 1 | 10000 | 1300 | £1,326,000 | £30,282 | 12 | 85% | £100 | £0.02 |
| 2 | 2000 | 260 | £94,640 | £6,065 | 8 | 65% | £70 | £0.06 |
| 3 | 1000 | 260 | £35,100 | £3,011 | 6 | 45% | £50 | £0.09 |
| 4 | 600 | 156 | £9,360 | £1,833 | 5 | 30% | £40 | £0.20 |
| 5 | 420 | 130 | £3,900 | £1,265 | 4 | 25% | £30 | £0.32 |
| 6 | 380 | 130 | £3,250 | £1,178 | 4 | 25% | £25 | £0.36 |
| Total | 14400 | 2236 | £1,472,250 | £43,634 | | | | |

| Assumptions | 1000 accounts per employee at cycles 1 and 2 |
|---|---|
| | 500 accounts per employee at cycles 3 and 4 |
| | 400 accounts per employee at cycles 5 and 6 |
| | 40% mark up for management and support |
| | Fully loaded cost per FTE of £22,000 |
| | PPH, promise kept rate and average payment value |

<u>Table 5.4 Cost per £1 collected</u>

*Service levels*

Service level measures are designed to monitor the coverage of collections workload. Typically a standard is set and actual performance is reported against that standard. Here are some common examples:

- Inbound calls service level – 80% of calls offered will be answered within 20 seconds. Data will be sourced from the incoming call distribution system.
- Inbound call abandon rate – 95% of calls offered will be handled by an agent before the caller hangs up, giving an abandoned call rate standard of 5%. Data will again be sourced from the incoming call distribution system.
- Mail received – 90% of mail received will be actioned within 48 hours. Data will be sourced from manual or automated workflow tracking systems.
- Manual work queues – Accounts queued for manual work effort, such as reviews by a supervisor, will be worked within 48 hours. Data will come from the collections system or from manual tracking.

*Call quality*

Responsibility for maintaining an organisation's standards of customer care does not stop at the point of entry to collections. The use of call quality monitoring as a performance measure in collections has become increasingly commonplace over recent years. A variety of methods are used from side by side coaching to remote monitoring. Whichever method is used the key points are to establish standards, capture evidence of what went well and what could have been done better, and give feedback to the agent who participated in the call. Feedback should be given as soon as practicable after the call is concluded where call taping is not in use.

Where calls are monitored in collections the observer is typically evaluating the following elements of the call:

- Corporate greeting
- Confirmation of customer identity to cover Data Protection Act requirements.

- Call control
- Information gathering
- Negotiation
- Summarising of agreement reached
- Call closure

As well as providing a window on training needs for individual agents, calls can be scored and data pooled to benchmark collection call quality and track the standard of customer care provided by collections staff over time.

## Performance measurement in Recovery

As mentioned previously, performance measures in recovery will have a lot in common with those used in collections. There is however a distinct change in emphasis. The work is tougher, so standards need to reflect this. Costs are escalating and vigilance must be maintained in the performance measures to guard against "throwing good money after bad".

*Attempts per hour*

Customer contact is harder to achieve in recovery. More customers are concentrated in 'no 'phone' queues and "he's not here" crops up in telephone contacts much more frequently.

Productivity needs to be tracked in recovery and one way to accomplish this, while recognising that an increasing proportion of effort will be on activities other than customer contact, is to measure attempts per hour. The components of this measure will be the activity codes registered against accounts on the collection system divided by the number of hours for which the agent has been logged on. Actions that qualify to be included as attempts might include account reviews, decisions made, directory enquiry calls or working leads to attempt to establish the whereabouts of a 'gone away' debtor.

*Cost per £1 collected*

This is the same type of measure considered for the collections operation. It involves apportioning the cost of recovery operations to the value of bad debt recovery revenue. Most recovery operations outsource non-core competences. Examples of this are the use of external debt collection agents who have a doorstep collection capability. It is vital to ensure that all costs are accounted for in recovery, where it is entirely possible for costs to exceed the value of recoveries achieved if the measurement system in place is not robust. Hot spots include doorstep collection and "trace and collect", where high rates of commission plus VAT make the net value of recovery, when internal costs of managing the agent relationship, barely commercially viable. Similarly imprudent use of litigation to recover unsecured debts can add considerably to costs without yielding any recovery benefit at all from failed cases.

*Other measures in recovery*

Of the measures discussed in the context of collections, the following can also be used in recovery:

- Promises per hour. Paradoxically standards comparable with mid-cycle collections can be achieved among recovery customers with available telephone numbers. With the relationship terminated focus on collecting the full contractual arrears has been replaced by the desire to agree and affordable payment arrangement which will pay down the recovery balance over time.
- Kept promise rates. Linked to the promise per hour paradox, relatively high kept promise rate standards can be maintained in recovery where the average promise values are typically lower than in collections.
- Call monitoring. It is important to ensure that, even though the nature of the relationship has changed, respect for the debtor and his right to dignity are maintained in recovery.

- Service levels. Tailored to the recovery landscape where economy of effort has to be carefully balanced against a build up of neglected ageing bad debt.

## Conclusion

Performance measurement is vital to the delivery of effective collection and recovery functions.

Measurement systems should be focussed on what is really important. Ideally they should extend from *motivating* productive and *effective behaviour* among collection and recovery agents right up to influencing senior management at the top of an organisation to maintain adequate levels of investment in the credit management functions.

How do I measure up against my competitors and peers? In order to assess relative performance and therefore best practice, benchmarking of the performance measures should be considered. There are a plethora of trade associations and benchmarking groups from whom comparative data can be obtained, whatever market sector you are engaged in collections and recovery on.

And finally, a tip for determining performance measures is to ask yourself the question: "Can I measure it and apportion a value to it?" If not, should you be doing it?

# 6

## Capacity Planning
_By Murray Bailey and Des Styles_

### Optimal resource

If the delinquency rises, business managers react by expecting Collections to work harder. Sometimes strategies and tactics are introduced to address a problem. However, it is more appropriate to be prepared and understand that it is a core responsibility of management to ensure that there are enough agents.

In chapter 1 we looked at the relative cost of agents versus write-off. The best Collection organisations are ones that do not view agents as an operational overhead. They understand that there is an optimal level of resource required for any given volume of arrears cases. We will look at this later. Initially we shall take the simple view that all agents work all cases equally. Once we have established the methodology, we will then look at how this approach can be extended and refined.

### Simple resource overview

"The optimal number of accounts assigned to each collector is a function of the average balance of delinquent accounts." This was the simple axiom that was applied at Citibank and figure 6.1

illustrates the principle. Auditing a Collections function included checking the average balance of each product and calculating the number of cases per collector.

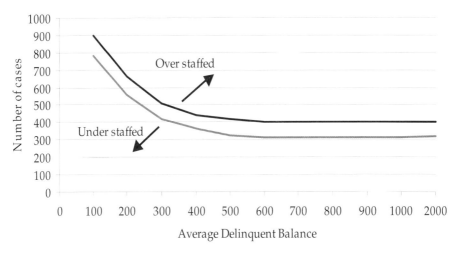

Figure 6.1 Simple staffing model

The appropriate staffing level was deemed to be between the two lines in figure 6.1. As the average delinquent balance approached $600, the lines levelled to an optimum range of between about 300 and 400 cases. The principle was that low ticket value portfolios, such as retail store cards, required fewer agents to work the same number of cases as a higher balance portfolio.

The issue with this model is that it was one-dimensional. There was no flexibility for greater or lesser efficiency. A company with a heavy reliance on outbound calls would be assessed on the same basis as one relying on dunning letters and outsourcing. The response to this is that if the operation relying on outbound calls was over staffed according to the model, then they should cut-back on the level of telephone calls and introduce less agent-intensive activities. This principle is correct, however it has one major draw-back: it presupposes that the model is up-to-date and based on optimal efficiency. It also assumes that the efficiency of operations is independent of country – which it is not.

## Collectors by arrears stage

To determine the staff level required we need three elements:

1. the number of accounts
2. the number of actions (reviews) per agent per day, and
3. the number of reviews per account per month.

From the number of accounts (1.) and the number of reviews required (3.) we can calculate the total number of reviews required per month. By dividing this by the productivity of agents (2.), converted in to a full month, we can calculate the number of agents required.

For example, if there are 100,000 accounts in collections and they should be reviewed twice a month on average. If a collector can work 50 cases a day (1,000 a month) then the required number of agents is 200 (100,000 x 2 / 1,000).

Let us first take the example of an operation where there are three stages of collections: Early, Mid and Late, which are based on the level of arrears. We will assume that the reviews required per account and the number of reviews by an agent are given in table 6.1. In this example the actions per account increase as the arrears level increases and the time spent on each review by an agent also increases (hence reviews per day decrease).

| Arrears stage | Reviews per account | Actions per agent per day |
|:---:|:---:|:---:|
| Early | 2 | 80 |
| Mid | 4 | 60 |
| Late | 6 | 40 |

Table 6.1 Example actions by stage

It now becomes clear why we have added the dimension of arrears stage. As accounts progress through the cycles, they are likely to require different action and become more difficult to recover.

If the number of accounts in collections is 60,000, 30,000 and 10,000 for each stage respectively, then the total required activity is given by multiplying the numbers of accounts and reviews for each stage. This is demonstrated by the calculation in table 6.2. To determine the staffing required to take these actions, we need to divide the reviews by the actions achievable by the agents. If there are 20 working days per month, then the actions per month are the figures in column three of table 6.1 multiplied by 20. The calculation is displayed in table 6.3.

| Arrears stage | Reviews per account | Number of accounts | Number of Reviews |
|:---:|:---:|:---:|:---:|
| Early | 2 | 60,000 | 120,000 |
| Mid | 4 | 30,000 | 120,000 |
| Late | 6 | 10,000 | 60,000 |
| Total | | 100,000 | 320,000 |

Table 6.2 Required activity calculation

| Arrears stage | Number of Reviews | Actions per agent/month | Number of agents |
|:---:|:---:|:---:|:---:|
| Early | 120,000 | 1,600 | 75.0 |
| Mid | 120,000 | 1,200 | 100.0 |
| Late | 60,000 | 800 | 75.0 |
| Total | 320,000 | | 250.0 |

Table 6.3 Required staff calculation

The total number of agents required for a 20 day month is therefore 250. This is an FTE (Full time equivalent) requirement and can therefore by fractions of people due to shift and part-time working. The figure is also prior to sickness, holidays, training, etc. Specialist functions should also be added, such as tracing and legal departments or external agency control.

The number of supervisors will depend on the role they play and the strategy of the operation. Some companies use supervisors as "super collectors". In this case, it could be that the capacity calculation already includes the supervisors. However, most operations will have a specific strategy, such as a budget of 10% of agent costs. Agent to supervisor ratios vary between about 8: 1 and 12:1. The higher the ratio means lower costs, but again, this could be a false economy. Productivity is the key ingredient to optimal performance and, as discussed in chapter 4, motivation is a large part of performance.

**Strategy segmentation**
In our example, we looked at an operation structured by stage of arrears. Increasingly, as collections scoring is accepted, departments are becoming structured around the risk of customers progressing to write-off. For each level of risk (profile) the strategy will vary. In other words, we should examine our capacity planning based on strategy since strategy drives the reviews per account as well as the time taken per review.

| Risk Band | Reviews per account | Number of accounts | Number of Reviews |
|---|---|---|---|
| Low | 1 | 6,000 | 6,000 |
| Mid | 2 | 48,000 | 96,000 |
| High | 3 | 6,000 | 18,000 |
| Total | | 60,000 | 120,000 |

Table 6.4 Required activity calculation – Early Collections

Let us take the example of a company that has implemented a collections scorecard in Early collections. The strategy is the intensively telephone the highest risk accounts and make no outbound call on the lowest risk accounts. Table 6.4 is an example of how the required activity might be with 10% of accounts in the two extreme strategies. Table 6.5 shows that instead of an FTE requirement of 75, the operation needs 78.8.

| Risk Band | Number of Reviews | Actions per agent/month | Number of agents |
|---|---|---|---|
| Low | 6,000 | 1,600 | 3.8 |
| Mid | 96,000 | 1,600 | 60.0 |
| High | 18,000 | 1,200 | 15.0 |
| Total | 120,000 | | 78.8 |

Table 6.5 Required staff calculation – Early Collections

Where strategies are applied throughout collections, the above calculations need to be repeated for each stage and strategy. However, the degree of complexity will depend on the volume of accounts in your business. If you are testing a strategy (a challenger), think about the impact on the number of actions and the types of actions per account. If it could be significantly different from the champion strategy, the capacity planning calculation will need to include the different tests.

There is also the question of whether the calculation should be split by unit, such as Outbound, Inbound and Administration. The answer is that it depends on the volume (for significance) and the operation's structure. If collectors have a specific role and there are enough to warrant capacity planning, then the calculation should be by function. Organisations that use call blending may need to predict the number of inbound calls on a daily basis. Typically inbound calls take priority over outbound, and the capacity requirements during the day and during the month will be important to the management of the operation.

## Optimisation

There is no one solution to setting the optimal strategy. Capacity planning ensures that management have a tool against which to benchmark performance. Using the capacity planning calculation explained in this chapter, the business can separate the three drivers: volume, strategy and productivity. Best practice capacity planning will have the flexibility to be updated as situations change. New systems may improve productivity and new strategies may change the number of actions required. Getting an accurate forecast of volumes is probably the hardest of all. In particular, accounts new to collections will be driven by the new business volume and strategy, account management actions and, of course, the economy.

If collections results deteriorate, tracking the volume, strategy and productivity, will provide management with an indication of the source of the problem. If staff morale is low and hence productivity is less than expected, making the staff work harder, will - at best - produce only a short term improvement. If the volume of cases is up, the solution is more staff. If the number of actions per account is not what is expected it could be that the strategy is incorrectly coded or (heaven forbid) not being adhered to. Problem solving in collections is covered in detail in chapter 14.

# 7

# Setting up a Collections Operation
_by Jonathan Day_

## Questions

There is no blueprint for the creation of a successful collections operation. Many factors influence the approach that needs to be taken. Is the operation intended to collect internal debt or an agency collecting debt for other companies? What are the commission rates or fees for debt collection in the marketplace? What benefits or disadvantages arise from the regulatory environment in which the debts are to be collected? What benefits or disadvantages arise from the terms of the contracts to be collected? These questions and many others need to be answered in order to plan the best organisation to meet the business's requirements.

If the organisation is intended to be a debt collection agency, the purpose of the plan should be to generate profits. In this way it is possible to undertake a cost/benefit analysis of each activity proposed to determine whether it should form part of the organisation.

Exactly the same approach should be taken to internal departments. In general, most internal collection departments are treated as cost centres by the revenue generating parts of an organisation. In reality, collections activity generates cash for the business, increasing profit and loss by reducing provisioning requirements and adding revenue directly to the profit and loss account by recovering written-off debts. It is possible to apply the commission rates and fees that prevail in the marketplace to the debts that the department is expected to collect, to arrive at a notional profit and loss figures that can be used in the planning process. This allows internal collections departments to use the same cost/benefit analyses as agencies. It also provides a more sophisticated measure of the department's performance.

In order to calculate the cost/benefit analysis it is necessary to look at each step of the collection process and assess the alternatives. One of the key elements of this is determining the headcount capacity required. Collector's wages are usually the largest element of cost within any collection organisation. The formula for calculating the requirement is this:

$$d \times c \div cph \div wh$$

$d$ is the number of debtors to be called, $c$ is the number of calls per debtor required to contact them, $cph$ is the number of calls a collector can make in an hour and $wh$ is the number of working hours in the month per collector, taking account of holidays and sick leave.

These numbers can vary greatly depending on country, age of debt, quality of contact information and technology used. It does, however, provide the basis for determining a key element of the cost base.

## The Planning process
The planning process should then focus on the key areas of collection to determine the most cost beneficial strategy: Over-limit accounts, Early Collections, Mid-range, Back-end and Legal.

*Over-limit Accounts*: The type of contact that needs to be made to these customers is, essentially, a customer service call of short duration requesting that the account is brought back within the limit agreed. In some markets and at certain times of the year the number of customers requiring attention can require significant resources. One possibility for the creditor is to outsource these calls on a flat fee basis to an agency. Other options include the introduction of shadow limits that allow the customer to exceed their limit by a set percentage without the requirement to call them. Standard letters can also be used to reduce the number of calls required.

*Early Collection:* Many creditors see this area as an extension of customer service and keep it in-house. With the expense of the systems and staff and premises required, this is a key area in which to determine whether this is the best option. Modern agencies can provide outsourcing facilities, where they obtain the economies of scale of handling multiple creditor portfolios, on a fixed fee per contact basis. Alternatively, consideration should be given to in-sourcing collectors from agencies on an hourly rate. This can prove cheaper that the fully weighted cost of employees and provides greater flexibility if volumes are likely to fluctuate greatly.

*Mid Range:* Volumes of accounts are significantly lower in this area but the length of conversations with customers, increases leading to a lower calls per hour rate. The collectors in this area require more experience and are more expensive. The considerations are automated dialling or not and whether to outsource. Agencies will typically charge a fee on the basis of a percentage of what is collected.

*Back End:* Volumes in this area can vary depending on the write-off rules in place, legal action policy and the number of accounts written-off in the past. A significant amount of negotiation with the customer is required to collect debts of this age. This means employing very experienced and costly collectors.   Agencies charge the highest levels of commission for these accounts, particularly if the debt has been assigned to another agency before. One option for the creditor is to sell the debt to an agency for a percentage of the total debt. This has the advantage of removing the debt from the balance sheet through write-off and posting a guaranteed recovery. The purchaser of the debt will, in most cases, be able to recover more than they paid. The creditor needs to make a careful analysis of whether the additional amount that can be recovered is less than the costs they would incur through the process of continuing to collect on the debt.

*Legal:* This area covers all ages of debt but tends to concentrate on the later buckets. The process in this area varies significantly depending on the legislation in force within a particular country. It comprises of the actions required to pursue a debt through the court system. The repossession of assets securing a loan and the calling in of guarantees and indemnities are also dealt with under this heading. Creditors can keep this process in house, using litigation staff and in-house lawyers, or outsource it to law firms and agencies. The decision by the creditor as to whether to keep this function in-house will largely be driven by the amount of activity within this area, the level of complexity of the legal procedure and the speed of the legal process.

Having reviewed each area of collection and assessed the alternative costs and revenues the creditor should be in a position to determine which areas of the process will be managed in-house and which areas are to be out-sourced. An agency should be in a position to determine which services it is prepared to offer to creditors. It is then possible to set-up the organisation.

The planning process, above, should have produced the raw headcount requirements for at least the following year. To this must be added management and supervisory headcount requirements. As a guide, there should be one supervisor to every ten collectors and a manager for every four or five supervisors. In addition, if the creditor out-sources business to agencies, there is a requirement for a supervisor/manager to negotiate agency contracts and measure the comparative performance of each agency. There should also be adequate administrative support for activities such as looking-up telephone numbers, banking collected cash, locating misapplied payments and dealing with product complaints where the loan is for goods supplied by third party vendors (e.g. double glazing, motor vehicles, electrical goods, etc.). Customer tracing is another area that should be given consideration. Whilst this can be operated in-house, many agencies achieve higher levels of success using methods which the creditor may not wish to be directly associated with! These agencies generally charge a flat fee for success. It is also necessary to decide whether to employ field collectors, staff who physically visit customers to obtain payments. These agents are expensive but, when well managed, can be very effective.

## People and premises

The next area to consider is how these resources are to be allocated. The most successful times of the day for contacting customers is the time that they are at home. In the UK, for example, this means before 9am and after 5pm and at weekends. This can be achieved in several ways. Some companies have agents who work normal business hours supplemented by an evening (5pm to 8pm) and Saturday morning shift of part time workers. Other companies operate a two-shift system, one from 8am to 4pm and another from noon to 8pm. This second method requires more premises, workstations and desks etc. but does have the advantage of providing the maximum resources over the lunchtime period when the most in-bound calls occur.

Premises are the next consideration in set-up process. Generally a call centre can be located anywhere and does not need to be in an expensive commercial area. It should have very good public transport services for staff to travel to work - this also attracts staff to the job. It should also be in an area that is safe for staff when they leave in the evening. Collections is not the most popular career choice and some companies provide additional facilities, such as gyms, crèches and canteens to make the job more attractive.

Consideration should also be given to the future. Can the premise cope with expansion? This is particularly the case with agencies where a new client may double the number of agents required overnight!

The selection of furniture and telephone equipment for the agents is important. The agents are the most important asset of the organisation and care should be taken that furniture is ergonomically designed, headsets and phones are comfortable to wear for long periods and chairs are comfortable. Even the arrangement of the furniture can make a difference to the way in which the agents feel valued by the business.

Communication requirements are paramount and great care should be taken in selecting switchboards and services. Many companies save significant costs by routing different type of call (inbound/outbound, local/long distance) through the service provider that offers the lowest call rate. Experience shows that, particularly for agencies, communication demand rapidly outstrips the initial requirements. As far as possible, all communication systems should be modular and expandable.

It is sensible whilst looking at communication systems to also decide on the collection system. These systems vary enormously in both cost and sophistication and the final choice must reflect the organisational requirements and the language spoken by the agents. If the collection system is integrated with the communications system, compatibility must be assured. Most modern systems are parameter driven and allow workflows to be structured in differing ways. The workflow and structure should be built to reflect the structure of the organisation. For agencies, care needs to be taken in selecting a system that can take data from many differing and incompatible systems run by the agency's customers.

Recruitment is the next major step in setting-up the organisation. The first recruit should be the operations manager. This should be someone very experienced in collections operations. In some developing markets it may be necessary to look for someone outside of the country. This person should be recruited at the beginning of the planning phase so that his or her experience can be used in determining the requirements of the organisation. It also gives this person greater motivation to make the process work if he or she has been involved in its design.

The next step is to recruit supervisors and agents. The level of experience required for each area of collections needs to be matched to those recruited. In developing markets finding experienced staff can be very difficult. It is possible to overcome this problem through training. The initial management and supervisory team should be trained by a quality external training company. It may even be necessary to purchase the programme on a 'train the trainer' basis if a local language course does not exist. Staff can then be selected by putting them through the training programme and selecting those who achieve well. This can be an expensive approach with as little as 10% of those trained making the grade but it will pay for itself in the results achieved by those selected.

**Training and performance**
Successful collections operations rely on a constant training programme. Staff turnover is generally high in this business and new ideas and methods are constantly being introduced. Regular training is important in keeping the efficiency and productivity of the agents at the highest levels.

Having planned, structured, equipped and staffed your organisation you need to be able to measure performance at organisational, area and individual levels. The majority of collection systems provide detailed analysis of the operation but it is possible to drown in the number of reports they produce.

At the start of the planning phase it was recommended that the organisation be treated as a business with revenue and costs, even if some of these are notional. The simplest form of measuring performance is to use the same technique. Using the information generated from the collection system it is possible to determine the revenue generated by each agent/supervisor who is actively involved in speaking with debtors. By then allocating the salary, costs of premises, systems, management and other overheads to each collector it is possible to create an agent level profit and loss account (P&L). When added up, all these individual accounts should equal the organisation's P&L. These P&L accounts can be used to identify under-performing agents so that additional training can be given and provide the basis for incentive schemes. The other data, derived from the collection system, can be used to understand why one agent performs better or worse than another but, as a standard measurement, the P&L account is very effective.

## Cost/benefit analysis

It is important to understand that different areas of the organisation will have different P&L dynamics. Commission rates vary with age of debt, some systems are used in one area and not another and salaries can vary with the experience required to handle different types of debt.

To set-up an effective collection organisation it is important to undertake the cost benefit analysis to determine what the organisation will do and what it will out-source, plan the requirements in headcount structure and systems, implement the plan and measure the results. Using this approach the optimal configuration of resources can be achieved for your business.

# 8

# Auditing a Collections Function
_by John Berkin_

## Introduction

Internal Auditors can have either a positive or a negative affect on our lives as Collections Managers. Which it is depends mostly on us! They have a job with responsibilities ranging from the simple auditing for compliance, with agreed processes and assessment of internal controls and process risk, to auditing for external compliance issues. The latter includes the Banking Code, statutory and FSA issues and external risk issues, operating as watchdogs for third parties from whom we might take in collections work for volume. In the widest case, they take on a role as internal consultant and process improvement advisor.

They also have influence beyond their weight. This is because, in the UK, internal auditors are a primary leg of support for the external auditors - their basic work is always relied on to some extent by the external auditors. So the better and more rigorous their basic work, the greater the comfort level and less the external auditors have to do.

External auditors have a different job, which they do on behalf of the shareholders. They have to focus on three different things:

- The arrears audit – asset and liability verification - have we got real customers and loans? Are they paying and under control? How real are our arrears accounts? Is there a hidden arrears problem (accounts waiting to surface, future cohort problems in a rapidly growing book, unrecognised and worsening debt quality problems in books which are closed or reducing in overall size, or simply accounts which we have 're-scheduled' to sweep the problems out of sight)?
- The P&L audit – are write-offs real and not under/overstated – are write-off rates as expected; are recovery rates what we expect for the necessary costs (and no more)? Also, do we have proper time matching between earnings and costs?
- The provisions audit (as part of both) – does the provision methodology work –are provisions real, sufficient and not manipulated – is the provisioning basis consistent with last year?

In this chapter we shall deal with the first and smallest scope of the internal auditors role – that is, auditing Collections and Recoveries for compliance with our agreed processes and policies. The question addressed by this chapter is what might the Collections Manager expect to see and where should activity be in a really well done audit?

## Our theme

Being audited is a 'getting and giving' process. And as is so often true in such cases, the more we give the more we get. If, as Operations Managers, we involve ourselves early in setting the scope and developing the work programme, the audit can be very constructive for us and not the annoyance, disruption and irrelevance it so often is. So the message is: get involved at the beginning, in the processes where the scope of audit and testing is established.

## The audit report

The Collections Manager must respond to the auditor's report. To understand the report we have to understand a little about the auditor's goals when scoping his work. There are two:

- To review and assess documented policy and procedure. To make an assessment about how well controlled collections and recoveries are and therefore establish what the risk to the business is;
- To assess how closely collections processes, policies and procedures are being followed in individual account cases, by individual collectors.

In the review and assessment of lending back-end internal controls and risk, collections and recoveries should be considered as a process or series of processes, almost as a 'black box'.

When making their assessment, both the internal and external auditor will take heed to the materiality of our line of business to the whole business. The audit scope will be trimmed accordingly, but with all process areas covered fully every three to four years in rotation. Regarding materiality, the key question is: Can our consumer lending collections ever represent a major risk to the overall business? How exposed is the business to arrears problems today and in the foreseeable economic climate?

Collections are usually material only to the extent our consumer lending is our mainstream income earner or asset. So, for example, if we are a building society our current accounts losses are likely to be only a small exposure when compared to our mortgage book consumer and valuation risks. They will not be considered material to the balance sheet and P&L – so our audit work focuses on process integrity and compliance, and will perhaps not be reviewed every year.

The work to meet the second goal can be very useful to the Collections Manager, supplementing Collections Department's own supervision efforts. Of course, if you run a very tight shop, sadly it will often tell you nothing more than you already know about internal collector performance and the effectiveness of each process. So providing good input for the initial audit scoping and work programme (by producing and sharing good operations data at segment, team and collector level) may move the bulk of the audit work done away from the ordinary internal detail and towards areas more useful to you. For example, providing additional insight into the performance of third parties such as Debt Collections Agencies (DCA).

The audit report will then contain a business risk assessment and, perhaps of more immediate application to us, the following as a minimum:

- Are we following the strategies and policies (and therefore are these written down) – timings, letters agents, and messages?
- Have we got systems and MI that are robust and accurate?
- Have we got systems that are failsafe?
- Have we got contingency plans?
- Are our policies, strategies and processes risk free within the limits of what is planned for the product, or are there weaknesses and risks?
- Are our key staff and managers adequate?
- Are we exposed to general fraud attack by any of our staff (through collusion or otherwise)?
- Physical security of data?
- Have we got smooth sensible roll rates and 'pots' (else process design is wrong or not implemented well)?
- Can we reconcile P&L and roll rate improvements to recent operational changes or customer risk quality changes (or to a particular tranche of business) that have taken place?
- Have we got DCA or software vendor exposure and risk?
- Are there un-noticed possibilities for collusion in respect of overdraft or credit card limit / spend-while-delinquent exposures?

- And whilst our Compliance Officer will ultimately be responsible, the internal auditors will comment on any exceptions they find to Data Protection legislation and Code of Banking practice compliance.

So the audit report is useful, not something to be feared, and should be accepted with thanks.


## The audit work

What do we expect in the second part of the work: the process audit?

Remember that an auditor is not a policeman or an active part of the Customer Fraud department, but for example, if they see something suspect about a too-close supplier relationship (with say a DCA), they must follow it up.

To save themselves a lot of detailed work later, auditors will usually get involved in pre-emptive work. They will attend some of our design meetings so they are aware without the need for much detailed testing, the quality of:

- New and ongoing collector training programmes;
- New systems and major systems changes.

The auditors have four tools: reviews, selective (statistical or otherwise) tests, external confirmation, and analysis and rationalisations. And in addition, they will be involved in the design and implementation of new systems.

The reviews will include our own manual reviews, the overall risk management model, previous internal audit reports and the actions taken in response and, of course, the external audit report.

Some words on confirmations – in an internal consumer-lending audit these will not be sent unless the audit scope memo recognises or suggests that there is a re-scheduling problem, or a large mortgage under/overpayment problem that has not been resolved by Collections.

The tests should be systems and compliance. Collections systems parameter set up should be examined for agreement with published strategies. The collections calls should be reviewed to confirm that they comply with the Banking Code compliance and Data Protection legislation. Specifically tests should include:

- Are there any collections system black holes (unworked accounts)?
- Do the actual strategies agree with published strategies?
- How effective is the Outbound collections call (probably crudely measured in comparison to 'one-to-ones' and tight collector management)?
- How effective is the Inbound collections call?
- Are there dropped or badly managed calls?
- How accurate is the incentive scheme accuracy and what is the propriety?
- How is debt sale/hand-off approved?
- The DCA interface: how well are money and costs tracked?
- How well is fraud identified and handled?
- How well are trace and lost contact accounts (risk) handled?
- How well are reschedules handled?
- Is their any unnecessary loss (through a lengthy or inefficient repossession and sale process for example)?

What should not be tested? The short answer is everything else. Four specific things that do not fit into the objectives of the internal audit are:

- Benchmark data and performance – as a good rule of thumb it is not the internal audit's basic job to comment or how well or badly we compare in the various benchmarking exercises. And they are probably not qualified to comment on relative performance and reasons therefore;

- Dialler performance;
- Our dialler management programme, to the extent that segments and portfolios are contacted fairly equally and no product or segment repeatedly receives a low priority to the overall detriment of its loss performance;
- Our letters and 'collections messages' and their tone and gradation (which we have already agreed with Legal, and with Risk from a portfolio performance aspect).

**Work which is missed more often than not**
The links to Risk Management and the proper working of the data feedback loop are often omitted from audit. For example, are write-offs properly analysed and fed back to the front-end to help set better policy rules or score segmentation? What happens to what we get to know about groups of our debtors during the collections chase? This information should be fed back for future benefit.

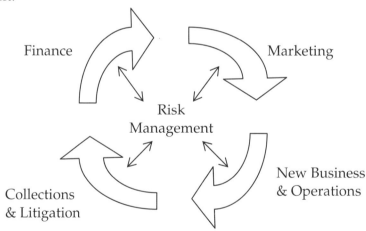

Finance

Marketing

Risk Management

Collections & Litigation

New Business & Operations

Figure 8.1 Closed loop credit risk management

**Beyond today's internal audit**
There are three requirements from Collections and Recoveries that are needed so the organisation can qualify (and remain qualified) for Internal Rating Based (IRB) status, thus minimising the levels

at which we have to maintain ongoing capital adequacy. These three requirements are way beyond the basic portfolio risk question of "how low can we keep arrears and losses" on our particular lending book:

- Is our contribution to the regulator's data warehouse of good quality and sufficient?
- How robust are our processes, including data gathering, if there is an economic change or shock?
- Under the tight definition of 'operational risk', what problems have Collections and Recovery had in the last five years, and could such problems be repeated?

Key to getting 'good marks' in this area is data analysis and therefore data gathering. It is becoming the responsibility of most internal auditors to follow these points up on an ongoing basis. So in future expect a lot more testing around your MI and data, and around your operational and Customer Problem Logs.

# 9

# Outsourcing
_by Kathy Cole

## Why Outsource?

The outsourcing of receivables management activity is becoming increasingly widespread in many sectors of the economy. Historically, outsourcing was undertaken on a partial basis. An organisation would maintain their in-house operation to manage and implement almost all of the receivables management and debt collection process, only looking to make use of an external supplier as a last resort. In recent times, a trend towards more complete outsourcing has developed, with the effective management of each outsourcing strategy becoming critical.

On the whole, the collections process can be extremely labour intensive and starved of capital expenditure, as there are often more exciting projects further upstream in the company process to spend the capital on. Added to this, even though all the cash may have been collected, the question remains; has the actual process been effective? The answer to this question could realistically be a resounding "NO" if collections could have been made earlier and the company has an over-stretched cashflow.

When debt is outsourced, staff can be released to undertake other projects. Many organisations are still driven by headcount ratios and, as sales ledger and collections management are labour intensive, reductions can be significant. Outsourcing can release valuable office space, as it avoids the need for investment in new technology and releases more capacity in IT departments as maintenance of older and unreliable systems is eliminated.

## Strategic advantages of adopting an outsourcing strategy

If Sales Ledger Management and Collections is managed by a specialist, who has the added benefit of an in-house state of the art technology system and a strong reference history for carrying out work for similar clients, the outsourcer can rest assured that they will get the best collections and early cash, along with quality management information.

In new business start-ups, where rapid growth is achieved, outsourcing eliminates the need for recruitment and training of employees, thus once again allowing focus on core areas.

For financial service organisations, a small improvement in collections performance can have a disproportionately large effect on reducing provisioning levels; this in turn improves profit and strengthens the balance sheet.

## Potential negatives and overcoming them

The main negative is the apparent loss of control of a core competency. But is control really lost? A small in-house capability can be kept to test in-house processes against that of the outsource partner.  Another way of mitigating fear is to have regular meetings to review management information. Agree in advance the information and reports required from the outsourcing partner, together with the required targets.

Choosing the right partner can, of course, be difficult and many organisations still have memories of outsourcing projects that have gone badly wrong for them. It is important to partner with a specialist company who will add value to your collections arena. The alternative is a generalist outsourcer. They will provide a reduction in headcount along with reduced costs, but at the expense of collections performance.

Who will make the decision in the organisation? Very often it is difficult to pin down the right person or group to actually evaluate and make the final decision to outsource. There are many reasons for this, including the fact that the most appropriate person to make the judgement very often ends up without a job if the deal actually goes ahead!

Although there appears to be potential negatives, nowadays it is possible to plan ahead and overcome these and it is certainly not stopping an increasing number of organisations seeking to implement their outsourcing strategy at a much earlier stage. But how should this strategy be implemented in order to obtain the optimum results for an organisation?

Firstly, you need to consider at what point to you should outsource; secondly, how should you go about choosing a partner; thirdly, what issues need addressing and finally the viability and evaluation of outsourcing.

## At what point should you consider outsourcing?

Normally the optimum time for an organisation to choose to outsource to an external supplier is dependent upon in-house resources available and the need to reduce costs and increase profit at that particular time. Also, how important is it to free-up more employees to work on core projects?

It is normally best practice, however, to evaluate the workload once two or three letters have been issued to the debtor, with back-up supplied by periodic and timely telephone calls. At this point an organisation can choose to continue to chase the debt, but this may take up valuable staff time and decrease the chance of making other areas of the business more profitable for the organisation as a whole.

The most economic point for outscoring is when the following is true:

**Recovery - cost of collection – opportunity cost < 0**

The 'cost of collection' is the internal cost to achieve the 'recovery'. The 'opportunity cost' is the net money paid by the agency should the account be outsourced.  The figures should be calculated using discounted cash flow (NPV).

**Choosing the right partner for you**
Organisations have definitely started to realise the many benefits that the strategic use of outsourcing can deliver, due to the fact that the addressing of budgetary constraints and improving of efficiency is very critical to their future success. The use of outsourcing allows organisations to focus on core competencies and by making use of specialist expertise, improved performance can be achieved at a much-reduced cost.  Potential suppliers now make use of the very latest in technology with regard to telephone and credit scoring, something which can be costly for an in-house operation to acquire.

Best-fit solutions allow the client organisation to choose when they want the involvement of an external partner and it is this concept of partnership, which is essential to successful outsourcing of receivables management and debt collection, (see figure 9.1).

The use of outsourcing can deliver improved financial performance, in the public sector, however levels of customer service are also paramount and it is for this reason that it is vital the right outsourcing partner is selected.

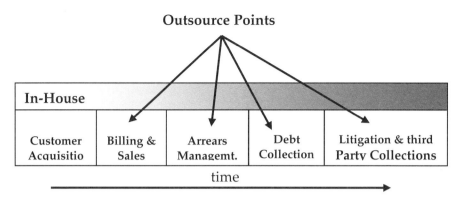

Figure 9.1 Multiple outsource points

**Strategic partnership**

The strategic partnership issues that need to be addressed are:

- Any organisation contemplating outsourcing should be happy the partner could genuinely add value to their receivables management and debt collection process by carrying out a complete overview of their organisation and its capabilities;
- References should always be taken out on any potential partner; particular areas to examine are financial stability and a good cultural fit with your organisation to ensure an effective, long term working relationship;
- Ensure the partner's range of services is extensive enough to meet all of your organisational requirements and seek a tailor made solution that precisely fits your requirements;
- Develop a comprehensive service level agreement to maintain high levels of customer service required to maintain your customer base;
- Set targets and objectives with the outsourcing partner that reflect the objectives of your own organisation and ensure that sufficient measurement tools and management information is in place to cope;
- When determining the cost of the process, consider the ultimate net return once the benefits of improved

performance have been taken into account, not just the headline cost;

- Ensure accounts can be tracked in the appropriate fashion and changes or potential problems can be addressed at any time. Clarify with the partner that they have an appropriate system in place, which allows proactive on-going account analysis by the partner with appropriate report feedback to your organisation;
- Arrange to have regular review meetings with the partner to discuss current and future business either in person or by telephone conference calls.

**Viability and evaluation**

If outsourcing of receivables management and debt collection is not currently viable, or if you wish to evaluate the effectiveness of your existing arrangements, then benchmarking with external companies can also prove useful. By transferring activity on certain elements of the process or outsourcing a small proportion of all activity to a specialist offering benchmarking facilities, a true measure can be obtained against best in class performance.

As the use of outsourcing continues to increase, the important thing to remember is that it is not an absolute process. By developing an outsource partnership at a chosen 'best fit' point considerable improvements in business performance can be achieved.

# Part Two

# Tools and Systems

"Collections and recovery treatment is like a puzzle;
an organisation must have all the pieces to get the
complete picture."

Kristopher Fannin, Labyrinth, Inc.

# 10

## Roll Rates and Probability of Write-off
_by Murray Bailey and Bayan Dekker_

**Roll rates**
There are two types of roll rate: Net roll rates and True roll rates. Net roll rates are quite crude approximations and are the balance at one level of arrears in month 2 expressed as a percentage of the arrears in the prior arrears level the prior month. In other words it is the percentage that appears to have rolled from one level of arrears.

They do not tell you what is going on, but reflect the net flow of balances through the stages of arrears. They do not break down the roll into what has not paid, what has paid and what has been brought back up to date. This break down of roll rates is known as the True roll rates. Figure 10.1 is an example of the balance in one level of arrears over two month-ends. Customers missing another payment have rolled from arrears 1 to arrears level 2. Balances have also rolled from higher levels of arrears, where customers have made payments. Customers who were two payments in arrears and made one instalment, remain in arrears level 2 while those paying more will reduce the balance in arrears level 2.

| | | | |
|---|---|---|---|
| Balance 2 down month 1 (Was) | | | £13,556 |
| Less | roll worse | -£4,270 | |
| Less | roll better | -£7,985 | |
| Balance rolled out of 2 down | | | -£12,255 |
| Balance remaining at 2 down | | | £1,301 |
| | | | |
| Add roll from 3+ | | £211 | |
| Add roll from 1 down | | £89,997 | |
| Balance rolling to 2 down | | | £90,208 |
| | | | |
| Balance 2 down month 2 (Is) | | | £91,509 |

Figure 10.1 Month on month movement of arrears 2 balances

This movement is demonstrated more clearly in figure 10.2. This is an example of a transition matrix, sometimes called a 'Was-Is' matrix due to the comparison of the state accounts were in and where they now are. These are the True roll rates from each arrears stage in month 1 to each arrears stage in month 2. The matrixes can be expressed as numbers of accounts or balances. Where numbers of accounts are used, the rows add to 100%. These are then the probabilities of rolling from one arrears level to the next in a month. This is multiplied by the original balance in month 1 to convert it into the actual write-off.

| | | **Is** | | | | | | |
|---|---|---|---|---|---|---|---|---|
| | % | UTD | 1 | 2 | 3 | 4 | 5 | Write-off |
| **W** | UTD | 93.5 | 6.5 | 0.0 | 0.0 | 0.0 | 0.0 | 0.1 |
| **a** | 1 | 71.4 | 13.5 | 15.0 | 0.0 | 0.0 | 0.0 | 0.2 |
| **s** | 2 | 47.2 | 11.6 | 9.6 | 31.4 | 0.0 | 0.0 | 0.1 |
| | 3 | 23.1 | 4.5 | 2.7 | 20.2 | 48.0 | 0.0 | 1.5 |
| | 4 | 11.2 | 1.5 | 0.0 | 4.1 | 23.6 | 53.1 | 6.6 |
| | 5 | 3.6 | 0.0 | 0.0 | 0.0 | 2.3 | 66.0 | 28.1 |

Figure 10.2 A transition matrix of roll rates

For performance and strategy analysis we really need a probability of write-off. If True roll rates are not available, the Net roll rates can be combined to give a good relative measure. The Net roll rates are chained together. If the Net roll rates from arrears 1 to 2, arrears 2 to 3 and arrears 3 to write-off are 12%, 50% and 65% respectively, the roll rate from 1 to write-off is found by multiplying each of the individual roll rates together i.e. 12% x 50% x 60% = 36%.

Transition matrices of True roll rates can be expressed over a number of months. For example the 'was' may be month 1 and the 'is' month 6 to give the roll rates over six months. Matrices can also be combined to provide a forecast of ultimate write-offs. Multiply a six month matrix by itself provides a 12 month estimate. Multiplying it by itself an infinite number of times will provide an estimate of ultimate loss. A short cut to this is known as a Markov Chain and will be discussed later in this chapter.

**Forward and Backward roll rates**
Transition matrices are complicated and difficult to track due to their size. A simplification is to track general movements in the form of worsening or recovering. Roll rates based on this simplification are known as Forward and Backward roll rates.

The Forward roll rate is defined as moving to a higher level of delinquency in the subsequent month. This would obviously be considered as worsening in delinquency terms.

The Backward roll rate is defined as moving to a lower level of delinquency in the subsequent month. This would obviously be associated with payback and would be considered as improving in delinquency terms.

Forward and Backward roll rates can be calculated as the percentage of accounts, from the total population, that rolls forward or backwards in delinquency. From figure 10.2, the Forward roll rate for accounts rolling from arrears 1 to arrears 2 is 15%. The Backward roll rate from arrears 5 is 5.9%. i.e. almost

6% of accounts in the stage prior to write-off either made more than one instalment or were 'cured'.

**Roll rates as a risk proxy**
Where a behavioural score is not present, roll rates can be used as a proxy for score.

In figure 10.3, as the proxy characteristic or piece of information, the maximum delinquency level in the last six months was used. In other words, this was used to determine the risk of accounts rolling forward.

In this example strategy, delinquency, time on books, ever paid and the behaviour score proxy, maximum delinquency in the last six months, was used to segment accounts. It would be expected to see:

- A higher roll rate amongst younger accounts;
- A higher roll rate for never paid young accounts than young accounts that have made a payment;
- A higher roll rate for more risky mature accounts.

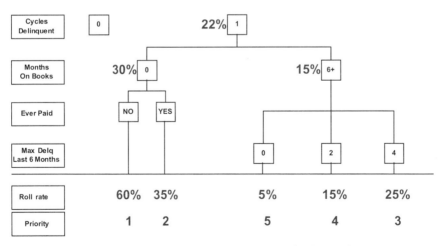

Figure 10.3 Roll rate used to stratify the risk

The example illustrates that the roll rate from up-to-date to Cycle-1 is far higher for young accounts that have never paid than for young accounts that have paid before. Young accounts, which display higher roll rates than mature accounts, which have never paid before, are most likely to go bad or roll forward.

Turning to the mature overdue accounts, those with a low score or a high maximum delinquency in the last six months represent a higher risk to the organisation. They are more likely to go bad or roll forward than accounts with a high score or low maximum delinquency in the last six months. This is reflected in the low roll rates for high scoring accounts and a high roll rate for low scoring accounts.

Roll rates can therefore be used as a proxy for a behavioural risk score to segment accounts into groups representing different risks to an organisation. These groups of accounts can then be treated differently. To illustrate this, a priority has been added to each node in figure 10.3 showing the relative importance that should be given to the various queues. There is a clear correlation between priority and roll rate. The higher the Forward roll rate, the higher the priority.

Figure 10.4 illustrates an example of Forward and Backward roll rates by strategy the Cycle-2 accounts. So there continues to be a close correlation between roll rates and behavioural score. Here scores have been divided into bands (or 'profiles') and assigned strategies.

Based on the roll rates, the organisation is justified in accelerating actions for the worse profiles, whilst decelerating actions for the better profiles.

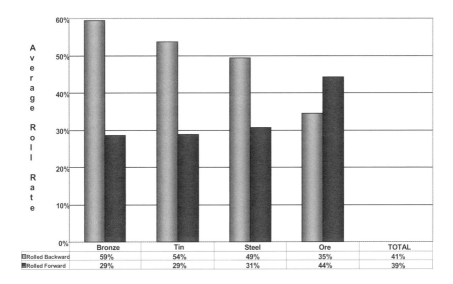

| | Bronze | Tin | Steel | Ore | TOTAL |
|---|---|---|---|---|---|
| Rolled Backward | 59% | 54% | 49% | 35% | 41% |
| Rolled Forward | 29% | 29% | 31% | 44% | 39% |

Figure 10.4 Roll rates and by strategy for Cycle-2

An interesting observation is that the profile range starts to diminish as the delinquency level increases. As the accounts progress through Collections, they become harder to separate in terms of Good and Bad.

It is clear that behaviour scores or behaviour profiles are not only predictors of risk, but can also be used to show the benefit to the collections operational department of the benefit of tilting collections actions by risk to prevent forward roll. This approach is explained in more detail in chapter 18.

**Markov Chains**
Now, let us return to the Transition matrix and our need to project future losses.

A Markov Chain is a sequence of random values whose probabilities after an interval of time depends upon the value of the number at the previous time. A simple example is the non-returning random walk. In Collections we can consider accounts rolling to write-off as the 'random walkers'.

The Transition Matrix gives us the probabilities of progressing from one level of arrears to any other after a period. Let us call this matrix T.

To find the probabilities of progressing from one level of arrears to any other after two periods we can multiply the two matrices together ie TxT (or T2). For three periods it is T3. For an infinite number of periods (n) the final matrix of probabilities (A) is Tn . A short-cut to finding this final matrix is the ultimate loss matrix A, which can be expressed as:

$$A = (I - T)^{-1}$$

What does this mean? I is known as the Indentity Matrix (multiply it by itself and it is the same!). Subtract the transition roll rate matrix from this and take the inverse (that is what $^{-1}$ means).

Most spreadsheet packages such as Lotus123 or Excel have matrix functions available for this calculation! The solution we are looking for is the probability of write-off, which is provided by the final column of matrix A.

However, a word of warning: because roll rates fluctuate, a single transition matrix will contain statistical variations specific to the period analysed. Chaining this matrix to infinity compounds these errors. Therefore the larger the sample size, the smaller the errors. Companies that use Markov Chains, may repeat the calculations every month to test stability. An alternative is to take a longer period or average roll rates over a number of periods.

We will need to use a measure of the probability of write-off when we evaluate the efficiency of collections strategies. We call this the Collections Efficiency Ratio (CER) and will examine this and its implications on tracking in chapter 24.

# 11

## Cost Effective Collections and Recoveries
*_by Bob Welsh*

**Where are we now?**

Traditionally, creditors of all shapes and sizes have set up their own Collection and Recovery departments to deal with the fall out in delinquency terms from their previously 'good' customers. They would invest in scoring and dialling technology as well as some dedicated software to try to maximise performance. They would then 'milk' every payment they could before assigning collection agents with a strategy very much driven solely to maximise recovery or cure rates. Very few however, invested in resource and performance management systems to manage staff productivity, performance and requirements, or activity based cost systems to cost collection and recovery activity.

Even with the best systems in the world at your disposal, the most traditional and important maxim of Recovery activity is: "Don't throw good money after bad". I am sure we have all heard this phrase many times, but how many of us take heed of it in designing strategies? Indeed how many of us know what our true costs are?

## Don't take it personally!

I have seen many strategies built by Collection Managers where the sole motivation seems to have been a strategy based on 'revenge' or 'punishment' rather than one built on an unemotional business decision. Sue him! Don't write off! Flog the account to death! I sometimes wonder how strategies would change if the question were asked, "If it was your money would you do this?" I guarantee one thing - the strategy would change!

## The trouble with scoring

Behavioural scores and risk grades are helpful when determining strategy and discriminating between debtor types but I am not sure they help totally in making cost effective business decisions. Good/Bad odds of 30/1 may seem good from a risk perspective but, in terms of income, if a Good account is only Good for £100 and a Bad account is Bad for £3,500 then you are losing money at those odds. I saw one system that formed a behavioural score and ranked accounts based on the percentage of the balance a customer was likely to pay. Great, you might say, 10% is better than 5%. However, this has to be balance dependent. 10% of £300 is not better than 5% of £1,000!

We need to make decisions and have the information on costs, and 'recovery potential' at account level to ensure that our Collection and Recovery departments are profitable and not bankrupt.

## The Collection and Recovery assembly line

I do not want to oversimplify it but essentially the collection and recovery assembly line has seven stages where costs and actions vary. In essence it looks like this:

- Collection low risk;
- Collection medium risk;
- Collection high risk;

- Recovery stage one;
- Recovery inc. Trace;
- Recovery inc. Agents;
- Recovery Litigation.

Not all accounts will go through each stage of the assembly line or in the sequence above but these are essentially the component parts, where costs and actions change.

## Time in the assembly line

Having established what your assembly line is, the next stage is to examine the time accounts spend in each stage: one month in stage one collections; three/six months with agents; four months to litigate and enforce.

Time in each stage will have a direct influence on overall costs for the stage. This will be important as you go forward, in order to cost strategies more readily and know the cost impact of extending or reducing the time in each stage.

## Unit costs and activity based costs

Unit cost measurement is a great way of getting started and establishing how cost effective your processes are.

Consider each part of the assembly line to be a separate department or business with its own fully loaded budget and volume forecasts. Ensure that the budget includes a pro-rata share of accommodation and other costs as well as a pro-rata share of management costs. So, if the annual budget for collection stage one is £1,000,000 and 50,000 accounts go through that stage each month the unit cost per month is £1.66 (£1,000,000/50,000 accounts / 12 months). If you keep accounts at this stage for two months then your stage cost is £3.32.

Do the same calculation for each stage but remember when you get to the Recovery Agents and Litigation stages you begin to pull in substantial external fees. Accordingly, the annual fee expenditure should be divided by 12, and then by the volume at that stage, to give you an external unit cost to be added to your internal unit cost.

Some of the best unit costs in Collections I have seen are around £1.50 per month an account and in Recovery £1.57 including external fees. Litigation unit costs tend to be in the £3 to £5 per month range because of the lower accounts to FTE on that side of the business and higher staff costs.

With activity based costing, this process is taken further and to a more detailed level, specifying costs for actions and accruing them during the account's life.

**What about income?**
OK, we have looked at the side of the equation that deals with costs of processes. We now have to look at the result of the strategies in terms of income to ensure we are profitable.

At a high level for the moment, let us assume that the unit cost per month in Recovery is £5 on average, regardless of the stage the account is at. Let us also take an example where, on an average debt balance of £2,000, 10% is being collected over 24 months. On the face of it this looks alright as we are recovering on average £200 with a cost of £120 (£5 X 24).

However, there is an opportunity to improve this profit and loss account. We all know that the longer we have a non-paying account on the books the less likely we are to get paid. Of course the longer the account is on the books the more we are increasing our costs as well. In the example above, if the account has not paid anything in month 1 our chance of recovery is diminishing and in month 2 may only be 23/24ths of £200. It should reduce in a similar way each month. Of course, this will never ever be such a simple straight line but we can use it to begin with to look at the effect.

### Income and costs together
Effectively each month the costs increase by £5 and the recovery prospects reduce by £8.33p from £200. The effect is shown in figure 11.1.

The cross-over of the lines on the graph show that, at around 15 months, with no payment, we have actually spent more in costs than we have the chance of recovering using the current overall strategy. The alternatives at this point are to outsource, write-off, or carry out a general review to bring the overall costs down. By automatically writing-off such accounts at 15 months you are driving out 9 months of costs and increasing the profitability of the recovery work on that portfolio.

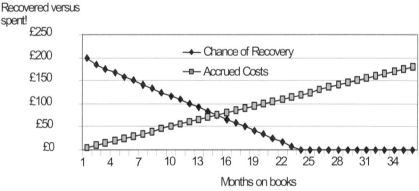

Figure 11.1 Assessing profitable debt recovery

### Breaking out the assembly line
The above example is quite simple but in figure 11.2 we bring in the total assembly line. We have assigned costs at each stage, know how long an account stays in each stage, and know the cure or recovery rates in each stage.

We do not only have the opportunity to look at the point where costs are greater than potential income. We can also look along the assembly line to see if we can reduce the costs at a particular stage, reduce the time at a particular stage, or even review strategy stage by stage to increase income. This certainly gives you a focus and a more business like approach to collection and recovery work.

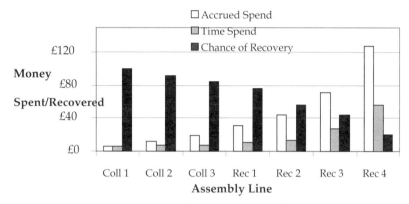

Figure 11.2 Costing the collections / recovery line

**Key indicators and markets**
Clearly the average balance of the debt you are chasing has a direct relationship to strategy, time in strategy and cost. The costs of a collector, letter or telephone call does not vary by balance, so low value debt poses considerable problems for Collection Managers. The cost income ratio for a bank or finance loan will look completely different from those debts emanating in the telecom, mobile phone, utility and mail order industries.

Accordingly these accounts spend less time going through strategies and a significant amount are outsourced or sold. Using cost measurement on the assembly line, recovery rates, and varying strategies by range of balances, opens the door to even better cost effective strategies.

The key indicators of the cost measurement emerge as follows:

- Balance;
- Cure rates;
- Recovery rates;
- Recovery timescales;
- Internal unit costs;
- External unit costs (Agents/Courts);
- Time in strategy.

## Get the software right

We have now got all the financial information we need but we are working on averages and still have quite a bit of work in retrieving the information and cost measurement.

There are sophisticated solutions out there that will allow you to import unit and activity based costs (ABC) behind every action (automatic or human) that you take in your strategies. This can range from the cost of queuing the account with a particular collector in a particular area, sending letters or indeed simply the cost of processing the accounts. This data exists at account level, so alongside the customer balance you are accruing the costs of dealing with the account.

You can now drive strategies based on whether the costs amount to x% of the initial value and truly manage this work as a business. Even better, each collector sees the picture of balance versus collected versus costs when looking at an account.

When determining strategies, in my experience this data is even better than the most sophisticated of behaviour scoring systems as it monitors our sole mission: "Don't throw good money after bad". We are no longer looking at the numbers game in terms of Good/Bad odds but at our own profit and loss account, and dealing in money! No business can be managed without a true picture of costs. Collections and recovery is no different.

# 12

## Integrated Systems
_by Kristopher Fannin

### Introduction
Within any given organisation, it is often the case that both collections systems and processes are separate from those of recovery. Consequently, a customer is treated in one system for collections and another system for recovery. In this type of environment, there is always a level of effort, maintenance and treatment duplication, increasing the overall cost of collections and recovery and often reducing its effectiveness. This chapter examines how risk-based, more cost-effective action can be implemented if an organisation moves towards a more integrated environment of collections and recovery.

### Collections and recovery
What exactly is the difference between collections and recovery? Collections is the strategy and process associated with obtaining receivables owed from customers who are delinquent, but still have active, revenue-generating services. Conversely, recoveries are the strategy and process associated with obtaining receivables owed from customers who are delinquent and no longer have active, revenue-generating services. Recovery

accounts are usually those that have charged-off and are no longer billed for recurring service charges. Collections and recovery is often viewed as mutually exclusive, with little or no systematic integration. The integration of collections and recovery, from both a technological and process standpoint, helps to ensure that all *treatment* processes and related *strategies* are integrated throughout the lifecycle of the customer. The integration of collections and recovery begins, first and foremost, with the integration of their respective technologies.

Full integration means performing all actions associated with collections and recovery in one system or piece of technology, rather than transferring a customer to another system upon completion of collections and the initiation of recovery. Basic characteristics of an integrated collections and recovery environment include:

- One system and/or interface that controls both collections and recovery for the entire lifecycle of the customer;
- One system and/or interface to apply treatment for different products and/or services at the same time for a single customer throughout all of collections and recovery;
- One system and/or interface that executes all treatment tools used in collections and recovery (e.g. letters, service orders, treatment history record, etc.);
- One system and/or interface to perform customer segmentation in both collections and recovery;
- A single reporting module or subsystem for collections and recovery actions, processes and results;
- All customer collection and recovery accounts will be linked.

There are numerous advantages of integrating both processes systematically. The most customer and business impacting advantages are outlined in this chapter.

## Consistent and efficient treatment

Collections and recovery treatment is like a puzzle; an organisation must have all the pieces to get the complete picture. Start taking away pieces of that puzzle, and the organisation begins to get a distorted view of its portfolio. In much the same way, when customers are treated in one system for collections and another for recovery, pieces of the puzzle are removed in the transition. It is often the case that only basic customer information is passed from a collections system to recovery system, usually in the form of demographic and current financial information. While an organisation can certainly treat a customer with this information, it is certainly not sufficient to be able to *effectively* treat the customer.

Integrated environments allow a holistic approach to the collections and recovery processes. Once customers reach the point of recovery, treatment can be determined based on previous treatment actions, payment history, risk classification, and the overall portfolio, both at the organisation and consumer level. The latter piece of information is becoming increasingly critical to the determination of treatment strategies and reducing the overall portfolio exposure.

To keep a competitive advantage, more companies are offering multiple products/services and bundled packages. A consumer now has multiple lines of credit with a bank – mortgage, credit card, car, etc. Similarly, a telecommunications provider now offers much more than local and long distance service. A consumer may now have local, long distance, cable, internet and wireless products with the same service provider. Consequently, customers may have multiple products in various stages of collections and/or recovery at any given time. A beginning-to-end collections and recovery system gives the organisation the ability to treat the whole customer, formulate appropriate strategies and reduce its overall risk exposure. Within regulatory and legal restrictions, an organisation may have the ability to expedite collections treatment for one product given the stage of recovery another product may be in for the same consumer. The collection and recovery processes, in this example, are working together because they are in the same system.

An organisation will usually execute a similar treatment strategy for consumers once they enter the recovery system as was done in the collections system. Rather than *building upon* the collections efforts, recovery often *duplicates* the effort. Rather than sending the same series of letters and calls in the recovery process, an organisation can devise strategies that are based on actions and results that occurred during the collections process. This determination would prove very difficult, if not impossible, in a non-integrated environment. Finally, there is continuous treatment when collections and recovery is done in the same environment. Inevitably, there is some break in treatment when a system transition must occur, not to mention the data-integrity issues that often occur with any information conversion process.

### Information sharing with partners

Companies are increasingly forming partnerships with outside collection agencies to assist with portions of collections and/or recoveries. This makes sound economic sense when an organisation can effectively identify the probable return on treatment, based on customer risk, relative to the potential commission payouts that would be required with outsourcing.

An integrated environment allows not only more effective use of partners, allowing the right information at the right time, but also give the organisation more flexibility in which segments of the portfolio will be outsourced. For example, a company may initially decide to outsource only part of its recoveries portfolio, only later to decide that it would be effective to also outsource part of its collections portfolio. In an integrated environment, this poses little complication, as the interface to the outsourcing partner is already established. In a non-integrated environment, however, a new interface would need to be developed, tested and implemented to allow access to the collections portfolio.

Just as internal treatment is more effective when all pieces of the consumer 'puzzle' are present, the same holds true for outsourcing partners. If an outsourcer is responsible for all or part of an organisation's recovery portfolio, more effective treatment can be performed with all the customer information and history available. If outsourcers only have the information provided to a separate recovery system, constraints are more compounded than those in an internal environment. This is the *only* information available to the outsourcer, whereas internal resources will usually have access to the separate system of record. A truly integrated environment allows outsourcers to treat the organisation's portfolio more effectively.

## Reporting and auditing

How should recovery treatment differ from that of collections treatment? Is your collections treatment as effective as it could be to reduce the roll rate to recovery? Would it be more cost effective to outsource segments of your collections and/or recovery portfolio? If so, which one or combination thereof? How effective is your recovery process relative to your collections process?

These are all questions that can only be answered by a comprehensive and reliable reporting and measures program. The pillar of any effective reporting program is the raw data that is available. A beginning-to-end collections and recovery system provides this pillar, as it provides information throughout the customer lifecycle, not just one portion of it.

With an integrated environment, a holistic approach to reporting is established. This insures a comparison of like data, rather than concatenated and converted data that is often compared between separate systems. This is the imperative component for seeing the entire customer portfolio and implementing appropriate strategies. In a non-integrated environment, functions are performed separately, data and analysis must be concatenated and is often missing, inaccurate or inconsistent across systems. The overall result is a more costly, time consuming, and more limited analysis result as compared to that of an integrated environment.

Within a fully integrated environment on the back-end, analysis is more easily performed regarding front-end processes such as marketing and credit policies. If an organisation reports on and analyzes an entire portfolio from beginning to end, it has the data available to identify potential issues with front-end policies and processes that are likely affecting back-end results (collections and recovery).

Legal and regulatory requirements affect most stages of collections and recovery treatment in many industries. Non-compliance and over-compliance can be very costly to an organisation – the former with fines and penalties, the latter with increased treatment costs and portfolio exposure. Believe it or not, organisations often repeat a treatment action in recovery that was already performed in collections for the sake of regulatory and/or legal compliance. This is often unnecessary. Compliance is not only more easily and effectively configured in one system than in two, it is also more easily audited and reported in an integrated environment. Additionally, a more reliable method of tracking performance and compliance with outside partnerships is provided with a beginning-to-end system.

## Cost of collections and ROI analysis

It should come as no surprise that the more complicated a system is, the more costly it becomes. These costs come in the form of development, maintenance, auditing and periodic change control. When an organisation has a fully integrated collections and recovery system, costs in these areas are substantially decreased. In addition to cost savings that are realised through a streamlined treatment process there is a reduction in required FTE end-users and corresponding training costs (i.e. only having to train one system rather than multiple systems). As discussed earlier, non-duplication of treatment and building upon previous collections treatment in recovery helps to reduce the overall cost treatment while increasing the overall effectiveness of collections and recovery.

Controlling direct costs (systems, actions, maintenance, etc.) and indirect costs (potential reduction of DSO, interest on the 'loan', etc) has a direct impact on collections and recovery ROI. The goal, of course, is to minimize the amount invested in the systems and processes while maximizing collections and recovery results. In other words, for every dollar invested in infrastructure, an organisation should expect more than a dollar recovered through the collections or recovery effort. If you have multiple systems/interfaces for both collections and recovery, these associated costs increase exponentially with the possibility of decreasing overall collections effectiveness. Some organisations spend a small fortune on multiple and complicated collection and recovery systems, only to see the returned benefits absorbed by the associated maintenance costs. The key is to keep the environment simple and powerful – a nearly impossible combination to obtain in many non-integrated environments.

Having the ability to accurately calculate an organisation's cost of collections and recovery is critical to evaluating the overall health of the program. A fully integrated environment allows for more realistic and accurate calculations of costs of collections/recovery, overall ROI, and for evaluating overall treatment strategies. After all, investing in collections and recovery tools will not deliver all of the available benefits if the organisation cannot accurately calculate and analyze the investment, associated costs and, ultimately, its effectiveness.

## Conclusion

The collections area is constantly changing in response to corresponding variations in industry performance, market trends, consumer behaviour and product/service offerings. As organisations are concentrating more on increasing efficiency and performance, while concurrently reducing costs and customer churn, there is a movement towards integrating the collections and recovery environments. Numerous advantages of an integrated environment have been outlined in this chapter. The bottom line, however, *is* ultimately about the bottom line – decreasing overall operating costs, while increasing overall effectiveness and return. All of these results can be realised in a properly planned, developed, implemented and maintained collections and recovery environment, building the case for integration.

# 13

## Using Diallers
_by Margaret Jennion

### What is a dialler?

Dialler technology usually fits into one of three categories: pre, power and predictive diallers. Pre-dialling software is resident on each collector's PC and automatically dials a highlighted number when the collector hits a function key. Power dialler software automatically dials telephone numbers in volume, and presents 'connects' to teams of collectors. A predictive dialler is also automatic dialling but predicts, on the basis of recent past performance, how long the call will last. The dialling is then paced to match agent resources. This prediction does two important things – it reduces connects where the party answers but the call has to be dropped due to unavailable collectors; and it minimises the gap between an operator finishing one call and having another available.

10 years ago, all power/predictive diallers used to be small separate standalone boxes, ready made for the job (Melita, Davox, Mosaix were household names). Not so now. These days organisations may operate shared software diallers combined with inbound call distribution systems. These combined systems offer greater flexibility and Internet integration capability. They

are comparatively new and have a relatively small outbound user base (most people still have hardware-based systems). The result is that the normal user-driven software development and upgrade process has not had much time to operate, leading to systems which are not yet functionally rich. The plan may be to upgrade the system, but organisations can find it difficult to recruit staff with appropriate skills to maintain and further develop these systems.

### The principle of predictive dialler usage is easy

The principle is that a predictive dialler-driven outbound calling unit is a cheap way of producing 'right party contacts' in comparison to manual calling. If it does not, it needs to be fixed. Or, if low volumes or a poor phone number base result in very low right party contact levels, it may be preferable to revert to manual calling!

Organisations often get very confused and lose sight of the goals and principles of collections and of dialling as a tool; sometimes it is considered a process in itself. It is not – it is just the organisational unit and a tool that works part or all of the process. The whole collections process is typically defined as 'early collections', 'impaired ability', 'won't pays and pre-account closedown'. It is worth remembering that our collections strategies are an assembly of customer contact actions and timings, and promise policies & processes which carry different weight with the customers – telephoning is just the way we do this cost effectively.

Management should appreciate that, for dialler management, the theory and MIS is complex. A dialler manager is like a good engineering officer on a ship. He does not have command but knows the theory down to degree level and knows every byte and every nuance of his installation.

There are some basic prerequisites to obtain high performance predictive dialling at a reasonable cost. There should be:

- A competent 'chief engineering officer';
- MIS which works, and is consistent with employees' time and incentive data and the collections system data;
- No fundamental flaws (such as not being able to bring forward yesterday's uncalled accounts to the front of the queue or queuing by a required sequence);
- A collector screen environment that works both for the collector and for the strategy designer. This means dialler screens that avoid the need to go to the collections systems for input of a promise, operator note or arrangement etc.;
- A pool of calls that is big enough for a collector to work on one kind of call (e.g. first broken promise) consistently for a one-hour plus period. Or a system which tells the collector the kind of case, the expected next action, the stage reached (or last action taken);
- Collections strategies for dialler calling which are well understood, hence not overly complex and not too many to be memorised.

Always expect to have and use a manual-calling group. These will ideally be equipped with pre-diallers. They will always be a 'background challenger' approach to calling but be used specifically for specialist types of accounts or specialist stages. Manual calling will be appropriate wherever volumes are low, calls are complex or data has to be reviewed before the call is made.

Seven to eight hour days are not conducive to maximise productivity due to the tight best-time-of-day windows and because that is a very long time to be on a fast paced calling queue. Therefore the use of shift staff with a minimum number of full time staff is ideal.

## Taking the steps towards high performance dialling

Using a step-by step dialler programme improvement process, it takes four to six weeks to get a marked improvement.

One of the main things to do before starting is to isolate the factors over which the Unit has no control. They should be recognised and the value being lost or destroyed by each should be quantified. Dialler improvement and management always has to be set in the context of what is achievable in the organisation and environment, to avoid unrealistic expectations.

Figure 13.1 is an example representation of the factors that will determine the success of a dialler programme. Early identification will enable the unit to focus on what can be improved, what is outside their control and how priorities should be set.

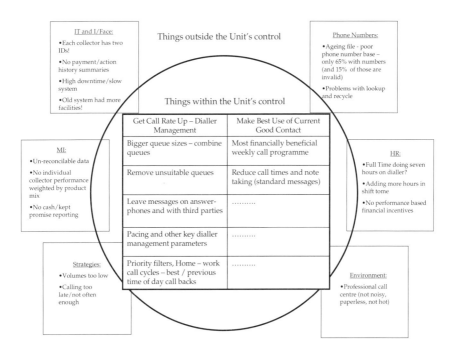

Figure 13.1 Things inside and outside the Outbound Unit's control

With the constraints recognised, the questions that dialler management should be focused on are:

- Do I have the right level of resources, at the right time to deal with the volume of work I receive?
- Are we calling accounts in the right priority sequence, on the right day, at the right time? If your customers are affluent and under 25 for example, there may be little point trying to contact them at home on a Friday night.
- Are the collectors being as effective as they should once contact is made?
- Is the operation itself running efficiently, without a significant amount of manual intervention during the processing day?
- Is my reporting detailed and accurate enough to give me an early warning of problem areas and guide the action I take to resolve the problems?

**Designing a system**

A properly installed predictive dialler is a large budget item. Getting the implementation and interfaces right is also expensive and so the business case has to be carefully considered.

Small organisations often have a lot of trouble setting up a decent dialler operation. A rule of thumb is: If you have not got a portfolio of 0.5 million-plus active credit cards or at least 20 thousand loan accounts or 30-40 thousand current accounts in collections, you will not see good dialler efficiency. The old collections processes with their specialist groups and manual calling (aided by pre-dialling) may well yield better 'effectiveness' results.

If development is planned, the following should be anticipated:

- Include a full two-way online interface in the budget or be prepared to abandon and replace your investment in due course;
- Be prepared to continually revise and improve your dialler MIS;
- Make sure the MIS reconciles to the collections system each month and is internally consistent – if right party contact increases dramatically, for example, the calling rate per hour should decrease;
- Invest in dialler and programme management skills for the management;
- Optimise the outbound dialling first. The best results will almost certainly be had, by placing inbound overflow only with a few designated, highly capable outbound staff;
- Plan to implement 'call blending' as a later step.

The outside world is not static and it is easy to develop a list of things which have affected dialler management over the past few years: the increased use of ex-directory numbers, a higher proportion of mothers going out to work, the increased use of answer phones and answering services, more variety in working hours, and the proliferation of mobile phones. Therefore, expect to continually evaluate and change your operational parameters.

Before either buying or developing a new dialler system it is advisable, if possible, to see the system operating in a similar technology environment, carrying out the same sort of functions and spend time talking to the staff using it.

Some functional shortcomings of new software implementations can be significant issues that should be planned against. These are listed below:

- The inability to schedule callbacks properly – either same day or another day;

- The lack of clarity over the minimum requirement for the dialler to achieve predictive mode – e.g. in terms of number of operators or time/account volume;
- No real reporting of call outcomes in terms of wrap up codes used to identify promises etc.;
- No proper tracking of daily account volumes and length of time on dialler;
- Inability to match actions to specific collectors to produce useable reports of effectiveness and efficiency;
- Cumbersome manual setup processes for each campaign, with restrictions on the combinations of phone number types (home/work/mobile) that can be used or the sequence in which they are called.

**Telephone numbers**

An issue that many organisations suffer from is that of the quality of telephone number data. Numbers are often obtained when the account is opened, but then allowed to deteriorate, as the customers move or change suppliers or as the numbering structure changes. This is an issue for the wider business to resolve, rather than for the dialler unit.

The clever organisations verify customer phone numbers at every contact, whatever the medium. The difference is quantifiable – those with good quality numbers may contact 90% of the customers they want to over a three-day dialler window. Those with poor management information will struggle to reach 70%. A collections operation does not have to be very large for the difference to be a significant cost.

As more and more of our customers apply Caller Line Identification, answer phone and other technology to accept only the calls they want to receive, the future looks rather bleak for telephony whether predictively-dialled or not. And the mobile phone number, possibly the most useful, is not reliably available.

Collections tools and techniques change constantly, as consumers change their habits. Predictive dialling will also have to change if it is to survive as the most cost effective part of the collections process.

# 14

## Problems and Problem Resolution
_by Murray Bailey_

**Delinquency is rising. What do you do?**
When I started at Welbeck Finance in the mid 1980s, there was a small recession. Welbeck had been out running delinquency issues by rapid growth. Suddenly there was no where left to run; the delinquency started to overhaul the new business and started to rise sharply as a percentage of outstanding debt after some five years of apparent stability.

We call this the Credit Wave; arrears take time to mature, so if new business is growing fast enough, growth in arrears as a percentage of balances is masked. The Credit Wave had struck Welbeck and the response was a typical one of 'all hands on deck'. All management grades were given 10 cases every day and expected to call the customer and obtain a promise to pay. It was a baptism of fire for me. One week on a job that was ostensibly to build scorecards and I was a collector.

From my own experience, most people are not natural collectors. Most people need training; an understanding of the collections process, the strategy, where this call fits into the series of other actions, the tone of the call, and of course, skills like persuasiveness, handling difficult customers, negotiation and so on. The performance of the management team was embarrassingly poor. It is also a lesson that has been learnt by many organisations and in some cases forgotten again. At HFC one director performed exceptionally well. He was responsible for the branch network and it transpired that he was farming the accounts out to the branches - probably not the most effective use of their time.

The issue with taking actions like these is that it is firefighting. It is acting against the symptoms rather than the cause of the problem.

There are many causes of rising delinquency. Fundamentally, however, the problems in Collections can be categorised into the following:

- Technological;
- Administrative;
- Policy;
- Affordability;
- Volume of accounts;
- Staffing;
- Productivity.

A classic example of the technological problem is where a new system is implemented and a work queue wrongly coded so that accounts receive inappropriate actions. In one bank's case, a large proportion of accounts that should have been queued for legal action had no action at all due to a simple transposition error in the queue number. It took a random audit, six months later, to pick up the fact that there were thousands of accounts in a queue from which no accounts progressed.

Administrative problems most commonly involve calls for direct bank payments, being late or not scheduled. Another example is actions scheduled but not taken, such as letters not sent due to a stationery shortage or postal error.

Policy problems are caused by the business implementing a new rule. For example, a more relaxed policy on restructuring loans by forgiving arrears will initially provide a benefit, but later result in higher volumes re-entering and rolling in collections. The introduction of a late fee, unless removed from the reported arrears, will clearly cause an increase by an equivalent amount.

Customer affordability is key to the ability to collect the arrears. The economy is known to have a massive impact on peoples' disposable income and something we can do little about. On the other hand, customer management and product design both have impacts on the amount of credit granted and the access to that credit.

The volume of accounts entering Collections is a capacity planning and forecasting issue. A rise in volume can be caused by newer business increasing its contribution to the overall book or all business. We will examine this in more detail later.

With infinite resources, all actions could be taken at the right time with no concern over issues like the proportion of a queue worked or contact rates per customer per month. The reality is that most Collections departments are understaffed, constantly running with a recruitment requirement. If the volumes are as expected and the performance to target, the number of people will determine whether performance deteriorates as a result of insufficient actions being taken.

Productivity is about measurement and motivation. It is often confused with staffing and volume issues, but must be separated for true problem resolution. Measurement and motivation are covered in chapters 4 and 5. Sometimes, no change can be the indication of a problem as much as a deterioration in performance. One bank implemented behavioural scoring for early collections and expected cash recovered to improve.

Recoveries did not improve because the staff were ignoring the scores.

Figure 14.1 is a flow chart of one process for solving a problem. Agree that there is a problem and give it a description or label. In this way everyone working on it has the same statement of the issue. The next stage is to identify all of the symptoms, potential causes and contributing factors. This is probably the hardest part. It is about gathering all the facts about the problem. Some of the 'facts' will be soft and subjective. Try and convert these to hard evidence, this usually involves data analysis. Look at what you know and ask "what don't we know?" Then find the answers to these questions.

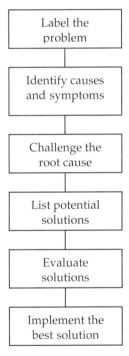

Figure 14.1 A problem solving process flow

To separate the cause from the effects, use any techniques that help you visualise the problem. Finding the relationships between elements can aid drilling down into the root cause. A technique called "Repetitive Why" is good for asking what the next level down is. It is simply a matter of stating the problem and asking why is this a problem and what caused it. With your answer, ask the same question. Keep repeating this until you have a root cause. Be prepared that this may not be the one you are looking for. In the real world, there is rarely a simple answer, however there is likely to be one main issue that should be addressed first. If you find minor ones, go back and ask whether they are still a problem after you have fixed the main one.

Other techniques include "Forcefield Analysis" and "Chronological Analysis". The former is a table of two columns. In one, list all the issues that worsen the problem, in the other, list the things that improve the situation. A word of warning: It will be very tempting to use this as a solution and rush into fixing mode. Avoid thinking about solutions at this stage - you are still trying to isolate the cause. The "Chronological Analysis" is a table of events in date order. Note the action, the date and what happened next. This will provide a timeline of events that often shows how intermediate actions made matters worse or clouded the true issue.

After identifying the route cause, challenge it to test that it is really the main source of the problem. If it is, list all potential solutions. This stage usually involves brain storming and it is important that no potential solution is rejected out of hand. People have a natural tendency to jump to conclusions. Listing all potential solutions prevents you from rushing off with the first idea and potentially not resolving the real issue.

Evaluation of the options will typically be from a financial viewpoint and with practical considerations. Solutions may be rated against criteria met and ranked or simply compared against one another using techniques like 'bubble up – bubble down'. Here solutions are listed and each one is compared with its neighbour. A better solution is promoted, the worse is demoted.

## Case study

A bank, let us call them International Bank, had a hire purchase motor finance portfolio. The delinquency was rising and to ensure write-off targets were achieved, emergency action was taken. Staff normally telephoning accounts at 45 days past due were used to increase calls to accounts in the first 30 days. This, it was argued, would reduce the accounts rolling to two payments in arrears. When a vehicle was repossessed after three payments were missed the residual balance was immediately written-off (a 100% specific provision). Further payments by the customer were taken as recoveries. In an attempt to reduce the write-offs caused by increasing delinquency, the Collections director decided to alter the repossession rules to successive missed payments.

The delinquency continued to rise and after a brief respite in losses, the write-offs started to accelerate. The delayed repossession had the main effect of delaying the inevitable. The problem was that this also meant that the asset depreciated further resulting in poorer recoveries from resale. Over a period of nine months, the loss per vehicle doubled.

The earlier Collections focus provided a very short term benefit. The cash recovered was higher, but the subsequent roll rates started to increase as the customers that didn't come to an arrangement at the first contact were the hard core who were then less likely to be worked at later stages. Softer debt was being chased and so the efficiency of the department declined (although productivity looked good).

By addressing a symptom, the Collections department exacerbated the problem. Delinquency was initially rising, not because of poorer collector performance, but because the number of new cases into Collections had increased and continued to increase. The cause was therefore new volumes in. The root cause was found by analysing the accounts entering. An analysis of the delinquency by time on books (a dynamic delinquency report) highlighted the issue. New business booked in the prior 12 months was dramatically worse than in previous years.

The business had done two things that impacted quality. The marketplace was changing; manufacturers were taking more finance business and squeezing finance houses towards more used business. International bank moved from 70% New vehicles to 60% Used within 18 months. Used vehicle finance was generally higher risk. Of the New vehicles, International had moved away from European to cheaper Eastern European cars. The net effect was a lower applicant profile. The New Eastern European car buyers looked like Used European car buyers. Table 14.1 shows the percentages failing the scorecard cut-offs and the override rates, before the deterioration and during. The Underwriters were compensating for poorer quality by overriding the scorecard and approving previously unacceptable loans.

|                   | Before | After |
|-------------------|--------|-------|
| % New Vehicles    | 40%    | 28%   |
| New Score Fails   | 8%     | 21%   |
| Used Score Fails  | 19%    | 37%   |
| Overrides         | 10%    | 20%   |

Table 14.1 The 'Before' and 'After' comparison of Underwriting

So, the root cause was not Collections, but Underwriting. The solution was to reinforce the original underwriting criteria and direct the sales team towards higher quality (albeit less) business. This process was assisted by improved dealer profitability models incorporating higher losses for Eastern European cars. In Collections, the solution was to return to the original strategy and to staff appropriate to the volume of accounts; recruiting people rather than re-deploying them to tackle the flood of new cases. From the problem solving process an improvement in the disposal of repossessed vehicles was also made. Someone had the idea of an agreement with a vehicle leasing firm who repaired and disposed of their vehicles. This arrangement meant a faster turnaround of repossessions and almost 12% reduction in the loss.

# 15

## Customer Centric Software
_by Gordon Crawford

### Introduction

The increase in the number of products now available to customers and the ever-changing economic cycle have significant implications for retail lenders. Financial institutions need to ensure that the levels of service that they provide embraces all the touch points for their customers. This is important during the initial engagement as well as later on if difficulties occur in the handling of accounts that are in arrears.

Research conducted by both MORI and Vanson Bourne show customers - and we are all customers - expect to be treated appropriately. When a customer is in difficulty, the accuracy of the information is of paramount importance; there can be no debate about the facts. When talking with a customer in these circumstances it is essential that the total relationship is understood and that the complete portfolio of account relationships is considered. It would be inappropriate to agree a repayment on a personal loan only to discover later that the customer's credit card was also in default. Equally, knowing that the customer has a savings account would undoubtedly have an influence in the way a decision was made about a debt. A customer centric, or single view, is therefore the only way of achieving this model. We have had customers with separate credit card and current account collections operations who have discovered upon only a brief analysis that 30-35% of the accounts in the two collections departments are the same clients. The opportunity for inefficiency and duplicate cost in this situation is obvious.

**Historical data**

To achieve such an approach it is key that software for the handling of arrears cases is designed with a relational database as an integral part of its architecture. It is then capable of supporting the many relationship types between customers and their multiple accounts, collateral types, third parties and related clients. The customer collections and recoveries system will need to support many soft data fields which enable the organisation using the system to describe their own types of clients, relationships, accounts, collateral types, etc.

In making informed decisions the assessment of risk is essential to the financial service organisation. The risk for the Collections department is: will the customer pay and if so when. As part of the process to make decisions it is important to know not only that a default exists, but to know whether this has happened before and, if so, how many times. Having this historic information enables decisions to be made regarding speed of action to be taken and the means for so doing. As a consequence there are major benefits of integrating the collections software with that running the recoveries. Whilst different skills are required the ability to be able to move a customer seamlessly, based upon the risk and previous history across all accounts, through the process will have a major positive financial benefit. Through the capabilities mentioned in the previous paragraph a financial services organisation implementing such a system has the ability to construct, and evolve over time as its business changes, a customer centric model that describes the risk in relation to the client. This has obvious advantages in terms of management information. In addition, the strategies supported by the software's rules engine are thereby also able to perform either account centric or customer centric activities. Strategies may be product centric at some stages of the processes and then become customer centric at other stages if the strategies are to be optimal in terms of both effectiveness and cost. However, in either case all information relating to the customer is always available for viewing by a collector.

## Deployment

Consideration needs to given as to the deployment of the solution. The practical use of these capabilities that are central to the design philosophy of an effective collections and recoveries solution can be constrained where certain options are taken for the software. If an organisation implements the software on one physical database and feeds all interfaces into it there will be no limitations in the use of the functionality. However, if for operational reasons the software is deployed across two or more physical implementations, on a departmental basis, practical considerations arise. In theory the same functionality is available, but in practice it will either be too difficult to use or will require varying complexity of interfaces and database synchronisation to enable its use.

There are implications in the way the organisation should be structured to achieve the most benefit. This will differ from organisation to organisation. On the basis that the only constant is change then a solution that can be configured to meet such changes is essential. This may not be an issue where all collection and recovery activity in the organisation resides in the business unit and there is no intention to share information or use common out-source partners to achieve economies of scale. Some of our US clients have deployed the system in this way because they already have sufficient scale and are not integrated with the other bank product lines in any way at the operational level.

Where the need is only to have a consolidated view of the banks total position for management reporting, it may also be an appropriate deployment model to support the operational running of the business. A copy of the data can be taken at the end of each day and a merged database created from the individual operational databases to enable the production of bank wide management information. Once again we have clients operating internationally across many different countries where this is the appropriate deployment model due to factors such as time zones, capacity and legal constraints in particular countries all coming into play.

All such issues can, in theory, be overcome by the use of interfaces and other techniques for making sure data is available across multiple databases. For this solution, the software has to have the same functionality and data structures. The downside is that the data may not be in the right place at the right time for the use required. However, businesses tend not to implement this approach when they get beyond a certain level. The reasons for avoiding this are:

- cost to implement;
- time to implement;
- cost to maintain;
- performance;
- data integrity;
- recoverability of data in the event of system failure;
- data security.

In summary the cost for the incremental benefit of the additional functionality can not be justified. This is despite the fact that the benefit would have been available at no incremental technical cost had a different deployment model been chosen to begin with.

**Practicalities**

There is no single correct deployment model for such a customer-centric solution. The most important issue is that the business considers its options and actions. If the solution is inadequate or ineffective, changes can be made, but it is far more expensive to change model later than get it right initially.

To aid the thought process, the following are examples where we have found that organisations can justify a customer centric deployment.

- Where a client is moved from collections into recoveries for one product, would the bank want to implement the standard that all accounts are triggered into recovery?
- When in discussion with a credit card client and negotiating a promise to pay, would it be useful for the collector to be able to see other accounts and their status? E.g. how are you going to pay as your current account is also overdrawn?
- Would it be appropriate to make an exception for certain common status situations such as deceased or bankrupt clients as soon as this status is discovered and move them to a central unit with common strategies to reduce cost and increase consistency across the bank?
- Where the bank wishes to out-source certain activities would there be benefit in moving them to the same process for this activity to reduce cost and attain scale to negotiate better supplier prices? E.g. management of the collection of cards from default card holders or management of collection agencies and the comparison of their performance across all products;
- Automated links to credit reference agencies can be technically controlled from one place and once again volume negotiations potentially improved.

## Benefits

Having considered the practical issues, what are other benefits from adopting such a customer centric approach? They can be grouped as tangible and in tangible - both of which have a major effect on the profitability of a financial services company.

The most significant tangible benefit can be the reduction in operating costs. Staff costs can be reduced by implementing a modern integrated collections and recoveries software solution. The extent to which an organisation automates the processes and decisioning via automatic actions and strategy processing is dependant upon the extent to which the company wishes to automate them and is very much impacted by organisational culture.

Other operating costs, such as agency commissions, legal fees, telephone costs and stationary costs can also be reduced. Agency commissions can be reduced by using the functionality/flexibility available to set up an in-house 'Agency' function. As a complimentary strategy, these organisations effectively pose as an external agent to gain the apparent third party impact of dealing with overdue accounts (a team make/receive phone calls and issue correspondence in the name of 'XYZ' Collection agency). Experience has shown that approximately 33% of accounts which would otherwise have been sent to external collection agents can be retained in-house and actioned in a low cost manner thus saving commissions on recovery (usually in the order of 20p in the pound).

Overall telephone and stationary costs can be reduced through improved decisioning. By taking the right action on the right account at the right time the operation does not waste resources on accounts that would have paid anyway or on those that are not worth pursuing. This is achieved through accurate prioritisation of risk via strategy tests and queries, comparison with historic performance data, champion/challenger etc.

Reduction in the bad debt charge stems from improvements in the effectiveness of collection, recovery and litigation activity – again, being able to take the right action on the right account at the right time. Such effectiveness is borne from consistent automated strategies, decisioning and availability of data to create and measure (champion/challenger) them. Experience shows that this is the benefit that organisations feel most uncomfortable about predicting (and thus tend to be conservative in claiming future benefit in cost/benefit proposals) whereas the actual benefit that does accrue is highly significant and more than proposed. Reductions in 'like for like' annual losses of between 5-12% are realistically achievable whereas experience shows that investment proposals seldom need to consider improvements greater than 1 or 2% in order to return an early positive net present value (NPV).

**Intangible benefits**

Improvement in customer service stems from the consistency of approach afforded by consistent strategies and the ability to understand the full customer relationship and take a customer centric approach. This includes improved control of risk by having a real understanding of the arrears portfolio, being able to forecast roll rates, delinquency, cost of collection etc. and understanding the relationship between arrears and the impact upon them of chosen strategies.

The customer relationship may be optimised by managing arrears effectively. This means that the customer relationship is maintained with those customers who can be rehabilitated (i.e. brought back up to date). These can be the most profitable customer long term and have considerable potential for further products and services in the future.

More advanced benefits include improved capacity and control. Solutions can be used to cater for greater fluctuations in volumes without losing control or having to make disproportionate investment in infrastructure etc. Additionally, staff can benefit from less exposure to mundane tasks as these have been automated and through the 'feel good' factor of having investment in systems made for them by the organisation.

An integrated customer-centric solution can provide better control and understanding of 'cause and effect'. This appreciation places the organisation in a better position to deal with changes arising from macro factors, such as rises in interest rates (and thus arrears levels), or micro factors, such as local unemployment. The organisation can swiftly change strategies to suit given that they can do so without recourse to the software house and also little involvement from IT.

The case for a customer centric approach is already proven and the financial benefits are being achieved.

# 16

## Open Systems and the Internet
_by Larry Stineman

### Introduction

One of the most important technological achievements of the 20th century was the development of the Internet. Most everyone is familiar with E-mail and the impact it made on both personal and business communications. Suddenly, written correspondence between business and clients takes seconds instead of days. The advent of the World Wide Web allowed any business, regardless of its size, a level playing field to market its name and deliver its message to millions of people across the globe. This new technology transcended borders and cultures and helped transform the world's population into a global community.

Equally important for the software development community has been the emergence and use of Object oriented design methods and the creation of open software systems. This design philosophy has enabled software engineers to create systems that not only meet current business requirements but also evolve and grow to meet future needs without requiring redesign and expensive software customization.

One of the last areas to implement these two technologies has been in the arena of collection software systems development. Historically, collection software systems have been designed and built around proprietary Client/Server software models. This design philosophy is still the basis for a large number of software systems on the market today. It is paradoxical that corporations around the globe spend millions of dollars on management seminars and consultant studies to assure that business strategies are flexible enough to address a changing global market but continue to accept antiquated software that is typically obsolete before it is even installed.

### Proprietary vs. open design - A software design primer

A proprietary system is by design, a stand alone, self-contained software system where any changes or additions to the basic package must be obtained from the vendor or by employing custom programmers to reverse engineer and change the actual code. Aside from updates that you may purchase periodically from the software vendor, a proprietary system will not evolve from the system you install on the first day.

To give an analogy, think of a software system as an automobile. Now suppose that you wanted to change the tires. This would seem to be a simple matter but in a closed system you would have to take your car back to the manufacturers repair shop where they would dismantle your automobile and replace the tires with the exact type that it had originally. If you wanted tires other than the original design, they would have to re-design the automobile to support these tires. The reason is that each part of a closed system is dependent on the other parts to perform its task. This inter-reliance means that a change to one part can cascade to a change in many other parts.

By contrast, an open software system is designed from the ground up with the capability of evolving to meet the changing requirements of your business as well as to interface with other software systems. This capability is largely achieved using Object oriented design principals. So what does this mean to non-programmers, and why would you care? Essentially Object oriented systems are groups of separate "Objects" that together make up the entire system. One Object may control all the access requests to your database tables. Another Object may control what language the system uses to display information, while a different object would control what currency the system supports. The beauty of Objects is that as your requirements change, you can replace individual Objects in the system, without replacing or modifying the entire software system.

In our automobile analogy, using the open system design, if you wanted new or different tires, you simply remove the old ones and install the new ones. That is because to the automobile "system" the tyres are merely an object. Take the case of the language object for instance. Suppose your collection software uses English as the language for all the screen presentations. What happens when the software is deployed to your branch office in Japan or Germany? With an open system design you can replace the English Language interface object with a German or Japanese Language object without affecting or changing anything else in the software system. If designed correctly, it really is as simple as pulling one object out and plugging in another one.

## APIs

APIs are the basis for dynamic customization of software systems without relying on the original software vendor. The API provides the interface between custom module and the software system. By "registering" the new module, it now becomes an integrated part of the system. Essentially, you can create modules that perform a new task not currently designed into the system.

To give an example, let us suppose the collection software system currently does not support a client interface module but you have decided that you need that feature. Your programmer would create a new module (the client module) that contains all the necessary user input screens and features you want. You then register it as a new object from within the collection software system. This expands upon the previous examples of replacing existing objects with revised objects.

## Open data formats – The software Rosetta stone

Another requirement in today's business market is the ability to share data between different software applications. An open data format can accomplish this. An open data format provides the rules a software system should use to accept or provide data when dealing with an outside software system. As an example, lets suppose you had a requirement to provide data from an account receivable system to a collection management software system. The collection management system would have a published data format that details the expected format for the information you were providing. For example, it might say that the file should be in comma-delimited format, and that column one is the debtors first name, column two is the amount of debt.

You would use the export feature of the accounts receivable system to format your data according to the open data format specifications and then simply import the data into the collection management system. This method of providing open data formats dramatically reduces the reliance on custom programming to link disparate system. Just as the example shows how to import data into a system, the same method is used to export data. If you wished to export information from a collection system to a third party document processing company, you would format your data in accordance with the third parties open data format. Just as Objects are linked to create software systems, open data formats allow disparate software systems to be linked to create complete enterprise wide solutions.

**Web-based or client / server?**

Client/Server based systems are made up of two distinct software applications. The Server component residing at a central location typically handles all of the requests for data, initial formatting of data and some of the data validation. The Client component is a proprietary software application that typically includes all of the user interface screens, initial data validation routines as well as some of the report generating functions. One of the drawbacks of this design is that if changes or updates are made to the Client application then you must install the modified client program on each and every users PC or workstation. You also cannot access the system on a PC or workstation that does not have the Client software installed.

Web-based software systems are designed to run on dedicated web-servers and are accessed via any web browser such as Microsoft Internet Explorer or Netscape Navigator. A web-based system can be accessed over the Internet or internally over a company Intranet. A web-based system can recognize individuals accessing the system and tailor screens and options to that class of individual (e.g. administrators, clients, agents, etc). A major benefit of a centralized web-based system is that, with the proper authority, users can access the system from virtually anywhere in the world, with nothing more than a standard web-browser. This capability is ideal for organizations that would have a requirement for remote client access, or with more than one location that needs to access the same system or data. Also the centralized design means that all changes or modifications are made to the web-server software and are instantly reflected the next time a user accesses the system. This eliminates the need and overhead associated with maintaining and distributing Client-based applications.

No discussion of Web-based systems would be complete without including security options that are available. Obviously any system designed to handle financial information has to be secure against hacking or outside intrusion. One of the most powerful mechanisms used to address these issues in a Web-based application is the use of SSL and Digital certificates. Some of the benefits provided are:

*Server authentication*: The server demonstrates to the client that it possesses the correct digital certificate. What this proves is that the client is communicating with the intended web site and not a site pretending to be the authentic site while attempting to steal information.

*Client authentication:* The client is authenticated to the server verifying that he or she really is who they claim to be. This protects the site from unauthorized users and hackers.

*Confidentiality:* Data is protected during the communication sessions against unauthorized eavesdropping.

In addition to using Digital certificates and SSL the use of firewalls on the web-server greatly reduce the chance of unauthorized personnel directly accessing the information stored in the database tables.

**Virtual call center**

A virtual call center is one that is capable of supporting agents or offices in separate geographic locations. There are several reasons that businesses are moving towards this model when evaluating call center solutions. One major benefit is it allows access to attractive labor markets without incurring the overhead of setting up an actual call center at each geographic location. Remote agents can work out of their homes or any area that provides an Internet connection to the virtual call center. Another benefit may be the ability to hire agents that are resident in an area that speaks a language that is not native to the country the call center is physically located in. This allows the remote agent to converse with clients in their native language, giving the appearance of an established local office. Also virtual call centers make it easier to match customers with the "right agent", thereby cutting back customer frustration and call routing times.

The open web-based system design provides the basis all of these benefits when used for developing a virtual call center system. Since the system is based on a web-server, customer data access is available to virtually any agent in the world provided they have Internet access. This allows the call center supervisor to develop queues for each agent, based on the region or area being worked. To the agent it appears no different than if they were sitting in a large call center, instead of in their home or remote office. The call center supervisor still has full access to all of the agent activity reports and notes, just as if they were physically located at the call center.

The web-based system design can also support multi-lingual requirements. Each agent would have a default language preference set by the system administrator. When that agent logs into the virtual call center system, all of the information is presented to the agent in the language specified for them. So you can have agents interacting with the system in English, German, French, or Spanish all concurrently.

Most of the discussion so far has centered on an outbound virtual call center model. The open API provision of the web-based system design allows support for in-bound virtual call centers as well. The API provides a mechanism for integrating the virtual call center software with different telecommunication hardware platforms. This allows creation of a routing module for received calls to any agent currently logged into the virtual call center system. For example when a call is received by the call center PBX, information about the caller is sent to the routing software module, which then interfaces with the virtual call center software via the API. The data for that caller is then routed to the screen of the appropriate agent at the same time the voice call is switched, via the PBX, to the Agents telephone set. The ability to use an open API greatly increases the capability to expand the system by providing the mechanism to interact with different software and hardware components.

## A specification for collection management software

Our goal at the beginning of this chapter was to introduce ways of creating and implementing collection software systems that would address the needs of a dynamic global market using the latest programming methodologies and communications technologies. The intention is to educate the users of these software systems in order to save them time and money when researching solutions for their individual organizations. We have reviewed the difference between proprietary and open software system design. We have demonstrated the necessity of basing the software on an open system to allow the evolution of the software to meet unknown future requirements, while at the same time minimizing the necessity of custom programming.

We discussed how APIs could be utilized to allow a software system to evolve and grow to meet future requirements. The discussion of Open Data Formats described a method that allows separate software systems to be linked into enterprise wide solutions. This allows data to be shared across the organization without requiring duplicate entry, saving both time and reducing the chance of data entry mistakes. Finally we discussed the benefits of the Internet, and by extension basing an open system on a web-server architecture, allowing carefully monitored and secure global access to the system via common desktop web browsers. As companies grow into the 21st century the ability to adapt to an ever changing global market is going to be key to its survival. The ability of software systems to adapt and evolve is going to be essential to any company's success.

# Part Three

# Scoring and Strategies

"Scoring evaluates everything you know about a customer and delivers a precise prediction of his future behaviour, instantly, objectively, and in a way which your systems and staff can immediately understand and act on."

Dr. Paul Triggs, INFORMA

# 17

## Understanding Behavioural Scorecards
_by Stuart Moseley

### Introduction
The mathematics of behavioural scoring is similar to that of application analysis. We are not going to discuss the fine detail of the mathematics in this chapter, but instead talk about some of the issues that one faces when constructing a behavioural scoring solution, specifically collections scorecards.

We will cover some of the traps that often occur within behavioural scoring, the tricks to avoid these pitfalls and tips on how best to approach a behavioural scoring problem.

### The big difference
The major difference between behavioural and application analysis is the data. Behavioural data has been gathered on the account holder by the credit provider using internal systems. As you are collecting real account performance information, you are not relying on application form data which is open to interpretation. Therefore you should have a greater level of confidence in your data than you may have for application scoring.

One further major difference between application and behavioural solutions is that no rejected accounts are present. Therefore, there is no inferring of performance to undertake. Thus all data is clean and should be consistent for all account data being analysed.

As the data is gathered internally, the range of characteristics available is vast. These include trend type data concerning the recent history of the account. For example, the following characteristics are quite common in behavioural scoring:

- Average Balance last three or six months
- Average Turnover last three or six months
- Highest / Lowest Balances over time
- Number of missed payments over time
- Time since account opened etc… the list is endless.

You should aim to cover all aspects of the account when producing any list of variables.

There is also a wealth of bureau data pooled from all credit providers. This data can be very useful in accelerating actions, as it gives as external view of the account holders to compliment the internal view already observed.

Due to this potential depth of data consistently held across all accounts, the Gini value (a predictive measure of a scorecard) tends to be much higher than that observed for application scorecards. Figures 17.1 and 17.2 are typical application and behavioural Gini graphs.

The credit provider can not only record all the behaviour of the account holder but the actions performed on that account holder also.

It is important that both sets of data be recorded. If no strategy information is recorded, a distorted view of the portfolio will be observed. Not all account holders will be subject to the same strategies applied by the credit supplier and thus types of behaviour will alter radically depending on what strategy has been applied.

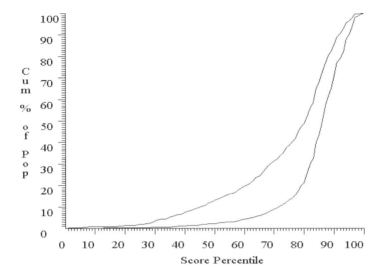

Figure 17.1 An application scorecard Gini - 36

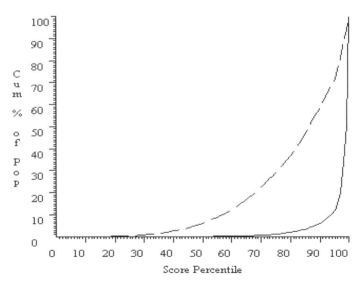

Figure 17.2 A behavoural scorecard Gini - 75

Not recording complicated previous strategies is the main pitfall of many behavioural projects – past performance will have an influence on how the account holder performs.

## Where do you start?

If you have a large database that holds a vast amount of data about your portfolio, one could have the experience of "kid in a candy store". With all that data, you can construct many models on a variety of different objectives; the key is to decide on the process you wish to analyse.

The usual starting point for behavioural scoring is the account management and debt collection area. A typical suite of behavioural scorecards for this area may look like the illustration in figure 17.3.

This chapter focuses on the Collections area but it is useful to understand where this process fits in with other behavioural scorecards.

Scorecards, strategies and analysis for Collections have the typical objective of predicting payments either made or missed. It becomes a question of treating your better customers better by not collecting too aggressively whilst the worse accounts are collected on quickly.

As with any scorecard or analysis, the main issue is to define the correct objective function or to put it another way make sure you are predicting the correct event.

One also has to consider if the analysis is to be aimed at account or customer level. You do not want to destroy a customer relationship and collect aggressively on the basis of one bad account if the customer has six other accounts that are all performing well. You may need to pool information across all accounts belonging to the customer to get a clearer picture of the worth as a customer.

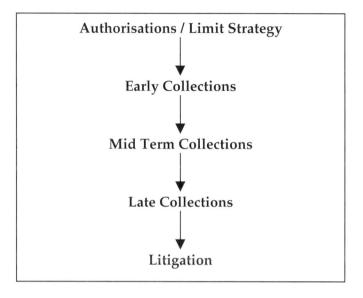

Figure 17.3 Multiple behavioural scorecards

**What to analyse**

With all this data and a range of fancy scorecards to predict all manner of portfolio performance, you may say to yourself "when do I start, this is too good to be true" but you must be realistic. You may be asking to develop a strategy to predict something either using too little data or worse still, the wrong data.

The sub-population you choose to analyse will have a large impact on the final analysis.

Let us consider a general collections model. You are sourcing the data for this development from one data file i.e. all information is held in the one place. The data for this development has the following information:

- Delinquency history;

- Cost of Collections actions;
- Time taken to recover monies.

Due to the amount of data available, you can predict a number of outcomes all connected to collections.

You may wish to look simply at whether the customers returned 'up-to-date' or not. Here the objective would be the risk only. However, the definition could be extended to predict consumers who both returned up to date and did so at low cost to the credit provider. For this solution, both risk and financial objective elements require construction.

These two models appear similar but will display very different results. The trick is to ensure what is defined achieves the required solution.

Realistically, the data may not be in the same place. The collections cost, time of collections and delinquency history information may all be available, but on separate data systems that are difficult to match together. The questions now become: *"Is it worth the effort of matching the disparate systems together?"* and *"Even if I do match the files successfully, can I implement a scorecard using information from separate areas?"*

So we need to moderate our enthusiasm to both keep our development practical and the implementation feasible. The issue of implementation will be discussed later.

**What's the point?**

Before you start to model, you need to know what the point of the model should be; what is the key driver or predictive quality we are hoping the development is trying to achieve?

Let us think about the predictive variable in more depth. What is the main objective of a piece of analysis? Are we predicting risk, costs, time taken for an action - so many options!   It may be best to take an example and work through some of these issues.

Let us use the example of an Early collections scorecard. Before we start to define the predictive variable, what does Early collections mean? Well, as long as you are consistent, it can mean anything you like. Let us say that we are talking about account holders that have missed one payment only - however, is this definition robust? No - this is not the end of this definition - this is another trap.

We do not want to include accounts that are recovering - i.e. accounts that are within the current collections path because of a previous month's indiscretion that has not been collected? Strategy has been applied to these accounts that will change recent behaviour so they must be excluded. Also, accounts that are in dispute where an account holder swears that he owes nothing should be excluded - this behaviour is atypical.

The full definition for the analysed population should be one payment down now, up to date last month and no disputes. Whatever the behaviour being analysed, a comprehensive and watertight sub-population definition is vital.

OK, we have defined our sub-population - at some length, now let us think about what we are predicting.  For this, we will firstly look at if the account holder pays up completely or not.   This is a pure risk assessment of the account portfolio.

A simple risk predictive or Good/Bad definition could be as shown in table 17.1.

Sounds simple enough…but is it? We still have some important decisions to make that will affect our overall analysis outcome.

| Good | Account fully up to date at the outcome point |
| Indeterminate | Account still 1 payment down at the outcome point |
| Bad | Accounts 2 or more payments down at the outcome point |

Table 17.1 Performance definition examples

Firstly, what is this mysterious 'outcome period' sometimes referred to as a 'sample window'. It is defined as the time between the observation point - where the account fell into our sub-population to be analysed - and the outcome point - where we apply the good/bad definition

It is slightly easier to see diagrammatically as is illustrated by figure 17.4.

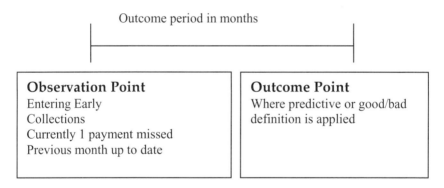

Figure 17.4 Outcome period

Unlike application scorecards, which have outcome periods of up to 12 months or more to allow a full year's life cycle of finances to transpire on an account, collections analysis can have quite short outcome periods. The time period again all depends on the type of scorecard you wish to build.

For a collections scorecard, you do not necessarily want to wait 12 months to see if an account recovers from one payment down, you want to show the recovery rate much quicker - but how quickly?

The assessment of what time period to take is based on a roll rate analysis. Figure 17.5 shows a typical roll rate analysis. The graph shows the percentage of bad accounts over time for our sub-population. Where the graph becomes flat, indicates where the outcome period should be set. This point is chosen as it shows where we are not gaining many more bad accounts and also gives a typical outcome period for most of the accounts to go bad. This graph is created for a few observation points to ensure the outcome point does not come from an atypical month. IN our example an outcome period of six months should be taken.

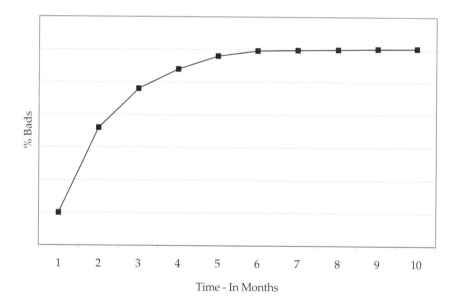

Figure 17.5 Bad rate over time

One final issue is to ensure that you have enough Good, Bad and Indeterminate accounts within your sample to produce robust analysis. A minimum requirement of the number of accounts in each classification for a single solution scorecard is as follows:

| | |
|---|---|
| Good Accounts | 4,000 |
| Bad Accounts | 2,000 |
| Indeterminate Accounts | 1,000 |

If not enough accounts were present in one month's observation and outcome period, several may be required. However, they must all have the same outcome period - it would be a shame to waste all that roll rate analysis to define our typical outcome period. Figure 17.6 illustrates the staggered outcome periods.

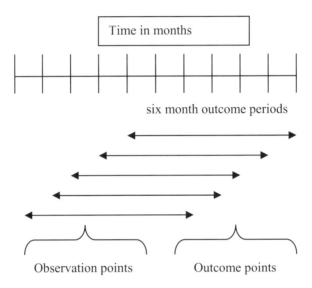

Figure 17.6 Staggering outcome periods to increase sample size

Before we proceed, we still need to understand one more issue and this is probably the most important of the lot - the previous strategy. Not all accounts have been exposed to the same strategy. This is sometimes not an issue when the strategies applied are similar, but there may be some huge differences between strategies - where does one draw the line?

If the strategies are similar, a pure risk model works very well and even if the strategies are quite different across the population, sometimes, a risk solution is all one can consider. However, with a little extra data available, we can create different predictive functions that incorporate some of the variations in strategy. This revenue model approach is covered in chapter 19.

# 18

## Collections and Recovery Scoring
_by Bayan Dekker

### Introduction

This chapter discusses the scoring technology used during the delinquency management stage of the credit life cycle. Best practice delinquency management strategies apply the most appropriate scoring technology, depending on the status and delinquency level of an account.

When creating a cost-effective and robust delinquency management strategy an organisation should: group accounts, segment accounts and apply the appropriate action.

Group accounts showing similar patterns of behaviour using the following available scoring technologies:

- **Risk Score** - predicts future delinquency levels of accounts defined as being 'Good';
- **Recovery Score** - predicts the payment ability of accounts defined as being 'Bad';
- **Credit Bureau Score** - predicts the risk and/or recoverability of customers at the credit bureau;

Segment accounts according to one of the following account delinquency stages:

- **Early Stage Delinquency** - missed payment of one or two required instalments;
- **Late Stage Delinquency** - missed payment of three or more required instalments;
- **Write-off -** financial write-off of the outstanding balance on the customers account;

Apply the appropriate collections tactic, using the risk/recovery behaviour group to drive the collection action according to:

- **Type** – e.g. letter, telephone call, SMS, handover;
- **Tone** – e.g. severity and content;
- **Timing** – e.g. immediate and delayed.

**Behaviour risk score**

A behavioural risk score predicts how an account that is already open will perform on a specific portfolio. In terms of the behaviour scorecard performance definition, the score will predict the likelihood that an account will reach the Bad definition within the next six months. This knowledge allows an organisation to use the score to make risk-based decisions on each account, for example, how harshly or leniently the account will be treated within the collections environment.

Table 18.1 is an example from a behavioural scorecard. Typically behavioural risk scorecards will contain approximately 8 to 10 characteristics. The above characteristics are typical of those found in behavioural scorecards.

| Characteristic | Attribute (Score) | | |
|---|---|---|---|
| Maximum Delinquency | 0 (38) | 1 (30) | 2 (20) |
| Months since Delinquency > 1 | 0-3 (23) | 4-8 (38) | 9+ (46) |
| Months on Books | 0-6 (20) | 7-24 (35) | 25+ (42) |

Table 18.1 A behavioural scorecard extract

*'Maximum Delinquency'* during a particular period in the past shows the extent of the delinquency on the account during the most recent history. It is intuitive that the greater the delinquency level, the fewer points should be allocated.

*'Months Since Delinquency > 1'* means the number of months since the delinquency level on the account was greater than one. Intuitively the longer the period since delinquency has been greater than one, the better the account is and therefore more points should be allocated.

*'Months on Books'* is also a typical behaviour scorecard characteristic. According to the life cycle of accounts, we know that the bad rate of a group of accounts increases until a certain stage where it levels off. This is because within immature accounts, the accounts that are going to go bad will tend to go bad fairly quickly. As a group of accounts mature, the bad rate decreases as the bad accounts are written off. Therefore, the 'Months on Book' characteristic is an indicator of how an account will perform, with more points being allocated typically to older, more mature accounts.

**Behaviour recovery score**

A behaviour recovery score predicts how an account that is already highly delinquent will repay in the future. Typically recovery scores are developed and used on accounts that are highly delinquent, that is they have reached the bad definition of the behaviour risk score.

The odds of a recovery score relate to the percentage of outstanding debt that is likely to be repaid over a specified period of time, for example six months into the future. If an account has a score that relates to recovery odds of 1:1, then half of the outstanding balance is likely to be repaid over the upcoming six months.

| Characteristic | Attribute (Score) | | |
|---|---|---|---|
| Months since last Payment | 0 (30) | 1 (25) | 2 (15) |
| Months since Up-to-date | 0-3 (38) | 4-8 (25) | 9+ (12) |
| Current Delinquency | 0-3 (40) | 4 (30) | 5+ (20) |

Table 18.2 A recovery scorecard extract

Table 18.2 illustrates characteristics in a recovery scorecard.

*'Months Since Last Payment'* indicates the likelihood of repayment in the future.   The longer an account continues without repayment, the less likely it is to repay in the future.   This is reflected by the allocation of more points to accounts that have recently made payments.

*'Months Since Up-to-date'* is another typical recovery score characteristic. The longer the period since an account was up-to-date, the less likely it will repay in the future. This is reflected in

that fewer points are allocated to accounts that were up-to-date a long time ago.

*'Current Delinquency'* is another common recovery score characteristic. Although recovery scores only apply to accounts that are already significantly delinquent, the higher the level of delinquency, the less likely accounts will repay. This is reflected by the fact that fewer points are allocated to those accounts that have very high levels of delinquency.

### Creation of profiles

As we know, scoring is a tool used to predict risk. A particular score relates to a specific level of odds or risk. The norm in any scorecard development is that the scorecard is scaled in such a way that the higher the score, the better the quality or lower the risk is. So for example, a score of 675 reflects a lower risk than a score of 600.

In order to use scores effectively, it is best practice to group scores into profiles that are easy to understand and apply. Profiles are used so that different actions can be taken on groups of accounts that display significantly different levels of risk. If scores were available between 550 and 700, for example, one would not wish to take different actions at each individual score. This would be impractical and too fine a distinction would have to be made. Instead, one would be more likely to take a set of actions on a group of accounts in a particular score range, and another set of actions on another score range.

Once this is complete, each profile can receive different treatment within the operational areas. It is important that treatment is consistent across operational areas. For example, it is important not to send mixed messages, such as granting a credit limit increase on the one hand, while simultaneously applying harsh collections calls on the other.

In table 18.3 we have an example behaviour risk scorecard distribution that has been scaled so that a score of 630 represents odds of 3,75:1 while a score of 645 represents odds of 7,5:1, and so on. Each score range has been grouped into score bands or profiles, and given a name. In this example we have 'Platinum', 'Gold', 'Silver', 'Bronze', and 'Ore' profiles. The level of risk represented by each profile can be determined, as the score to odds relationship is known for this scorecard. As an illustration, the 'Silver' profile equates to accounts with odds of 15:1 to just less than 30:1. This is the group of accounts that score between 660 and 674. Grouping scores into profiles simplifies the use of scores, as the groups are formed according to known levels of risk and are more understandable than a wide range of scores. Practical use of profiles within strategies is also simpler and easier to understand than the use of scores.

| Score | Profile | Odds |
|-------|---------|------|
| 690+ | Platinum | 60:1+ |
| 675 – 689 | Gold | 30:1 - < 60:1 |
| 660 – 674 | Silver | 15:1 - < 30:1 |
| 645 – 659 | Bronze | 7.5:1 - <15:1 |
| 630 – 644 | Ore | 3.75:1 - < 7.5:1 |
| : | : | : |

Table 18.3 Risk score profiles

In table 18.4 we have an example recovery scorecard distribution. As previously described, recovery scores are built to predict the likelihood or projected percentage of balance that will be repaid in a particular period into the future.

This scorecard has been scaled so that a score of 200 represents a predicted repayment of 20% or odds of 0,25:1. A score of 240 represents a predicted repayment of 50% or odds of 1:1. Again, as with the behaviour risk score, the scores have been grouped into profiles, and have been named, in order to make them more easily understandable and more easily utilised within the collections strategy. In this example the 'Silver' profile, which refers to the score band of 200 – 219, equates to recovery percentages of 20% - just less than 30%. That is, odds of recovery of 0.25:1 to 0.43:1.

| Score | Profile | Recovery % |
|:---:|:---:|:---:|
| 240+ | Platinum | 50%+ |
| 220 – 240 | Gold | 30% - < 50% |
| 200 – 220 | Silver | 20% - < 30% |
| 180 – 200 | Bronze | 10% - <20% |
| 160 – 180 | Ore | 5% - < 10% |
| : | : | : |

Table 18.4 Recovery score profiles

**Proxies for risk and recovery prediction**
Scores will always give more predictive power than the use of proxies, as they are statistically and empirically derived. In a scorecard a combination of characteristics are used, which are correctly weighted to take into account the interrelationships (correlation) between individual characteristics.

When scores are unavailable, other predictive information can be used as proxies for scores. Characteristics can be used as alternatives for scores when we know that these pieces of information are highly predictive.

Examples of characteristics that can be used as proxies for behaviour risk scores to predict the likelihood of an account reaching a certain level of delinquency include:

■ Maximum delinquency during the last 6-12 months, as the higher the delinquency the higher the expected future risk;

- Number of times delinquent in the last 6-12 months, as the greater the number of times delinquent, the higher the potential risk;
- Months since last delinquency, as the longer the period since the last delinquency, the lower the projected risk;
- Months since maximum delinquency, as the greater the period since maximum delinquency, the lower the anticipated risk.

Examples of characteristics that can be used as alternatives for recovery scores include:

- Payments as a percentage of balance over the last six months, as the higher the % the greater the likelihood of repayment;
- Months since significant payment made, as the greater the period since significant payment the lower the likelihood of future payments;
- Number of payments made in the last six months, as the greater the number of repayments the greater the probability of further payments.

**Credit bureau scores**

Credit bureau scores were developed in the U.S. in the 1980s and have become standard industry practice for both application and ongoing account management. A Credit Bureau score is developed on pooled data, provided by all contributing credit grantors. Characteristics are based on payments, usage and delinquency across all accounts that an individual has. Expressed as a score, this enables an organisation to have an industry-wide, global view of the credit risk and predicted future performance of a customer. The Credit Bureau score is dynamic and changes according to the individual's behaviour on all of their reported accounts.

Credit Bureau scores not only assist in the initial granting of credit, but also the ongoing management of a customers risk. For example, a possible early warning of future delinquency is when a customer is performing well with the organisation in question but is performing poorly with other lenders, based on their Credit Bureau score.

In the same way that application scores can be cross-matrixed (dual score matrix) with Credit Bureau scores, splitting out and analysing each behaviour score range by credit bureau score adds to overall predictive power. Table 18.5 shows the odds for each cell of the matrix.

| | | Credit Bureau Scores | | | | |
|---|---|---|---|---|---|---|
| | Avg Odds | Very Low | Low | Medium | High | Very High |
| Behaviour Score | | | | | | |
| 660 | 15 / 1 | 8.5 / 1 | 11.75 / 1 | 15 / 1 | 22 / 1 | 31 / 1 |

Table 18.5 Combining risk and bureau scores

Dual scoring can be applied to all areas of account management and brings additional business benefit when used correctly. Table 18.6 illustrates how a dual matrix approach would be applied in a delinquent collections strategy.

| BEHAVIOUR SCORE | LOW BUREAU SCORE | MEDIUM BUREAU SCORE | HIGH BUREAU SCORE |
|---|---|---|---|
| LOW (HIGH RISK) | Early legal or collection agency | Accelerate effort or early closure | Standard collection practice |
| MEDIUM (MARGINAL RISK) | Accelerate effort or early closure | Standard collection practice | Delay work queue entry date or account closure |
| HIGH (GOOD RISK) | Standard collection practice | Delay work queue entry date or account closure | "Super" decelerated treatment |

Table 18.6 Collection strategies for the risk/bureau score matrix

When using dual scores in account management strategies, it is very important to consider the age of the Credit Bureau score, as the score's predictive power tends to decline over time. A behaviour score is dynamic and is typically calculated on a monthly basis and is therefore always up-to-date. A Credit Bureau score is typically refreshed on a quarterly basis via an off-line batch procedure with accounts sent to the credit bureau for scoring. In many countries, the yearly FatMAN schedule has become the standard with batch refreshes in February, May, August and November.

# 19

## Revenue Models
_by Stuart Moseley_

### The revenue model

In chapter 17 we examined behavioural scorecards. These provide a risk dimension. If financial information is available, the predictive function of models can now include elements such as revenue and time.

We shall delve a little further into the revenue model and investigate the advantages and problems of this approach compared to a traditional risk model.

Further to the strict discrete Good/Bad or Pay/No pay prediction, you can create many other types of analysis. A continuous decision variable – where the predictive variable takes a range, is a very useful tool in behavioural analysis.   Financial data allows this type of objective to be achieved.

Step-wise linear regression is especially good at predicting across a continuous variable. A revenue model is designed to predict the amount of profit or loss one collects on an account, and is especially good in incorporating some of the elements of the previous strategy decision.

Let us define the predictive variable for the revenue model as follows:

**(Money received) – (Money spent) = Revenue**

This calculation is again to be made at the outcome point.

It is best to discuss the merits of the revenue model for complicated previous strategies with an example.

We will investigate two types of previous strategy applied at the observation points – one simple and one more complicated – and see how this affects the approach to the modelling of the two predictive functions.

Firstly let's get the difficult, complicated strategy out of the way.

Suppose the previous collections strategy entailed splitting the population into four groups dependant on score. The strategies and costs applied to these risk grades vary greatly.  Table 16.1 illustrates this.

| Risk Grade based on Score | Cost |
|---|---|
| Low 45% of population | £5.00 |
| Medium 35% of population | £20.00 |
| High 15% of population | £70.00 |
| Very High 5% of population | £150.00 |

Table 19.1 Collection cost by strategy

Now we have to get hypothetical to further understand the merits of the revenue scorecard over the risk scorecard.

In a risk scorecard, it does not matter how much money is laid out to collect the debt, if the account holder pays up, they are good - there may be a slight flaw in this argument though.

Let us take four accounts as an example: two low risk and two very high risk accounts. Table 19.2 illustrates how the risk assessment would assign them.

| Account Number | Outcome behaviour | Risk Rating (Good/Bad) | Cost to collect |
|---|---|---|---|
| 1 - Low Risk | Recovered | Good | £5.00 |
| 2 - Low Risk | Did not recover | Bad | £5.00 |
| 3 - Very High Risk | Recovered | Good | £150.00 |
| 4 - Very High Risk | Did not recover | Bad | £150.00 |

Table 19.2 Outcome assignment based on risk

"What's wrong with that?" you may ask. Well, is it correct to assign an account Bad if they are exposed to a very soft strategy? They may have reacted differently if they had been exposed to a harsher strategy that worked for account three. So where does that leave us? Unless we have a crystal ball, we will not know the answer.

We could look at the problem like this; account four is much worse than account two as more resource has been thrown at the collection of this debt but they both are still bad. Does this mean we have to create a new category in the risk Good/Bad definition of 'extremely bad'? Well, not really. Discrete models need a "yes/no" decision.

We can however analyse this by comparing how much money was laid out to collect on the account compared to how much we received - i.e. the revenue model.

This levels the playing field for all accounts and allows things like account four to appear really bad whilst account two appears less bad - more indeterminate as all accounts have a monetary value of revenue attached to them.

Table 19.3 illustrates a slightly simpler collections strategy - just two this time. This time, luckily, the strategies are very similar in cost and thus if an account recovers or not is a much more useful predictive measure than in the previous example. Thus a risk model would be both appropriate and predictive.

| Risk Grade based on Score | Cost |
|---|---|
| Low 60% of population | £5.00 |
| Medium 40% of population | £10.00 |

Table 19.3 A simple strategy for outcome assignment

Before we complete our glorious analysis, we need to ensure that all variables to be analysed can be implemented. Only introduce variables to your model that are either available now or can be obtained with little extra work. The last thing one wants after all the hard work is a scorecard that is impossible to implement.

With any scorecard, monitoring is of the utmost importance. The scorecards should be checked very regularly because they can easily shift with changes in strategy. If you keep an eye on the population portfolio and slightly re-align the scorecard when strategy or population changes occur, the models will stay more predictive for longer.

## Conclusions

So what have we learnt? Well, there is more to behavioural scoring than one might first imagine.

There are many traps and pitfalls to be negotiated, but if the analysis is set out correctly and a clear description of what you need to achieve is known, the waters should be smooth.

Know what you want and keep in mind that you may need to bend your objective to fit the available data but overlook the previous strategy activity at your peril.

The behaviour of the customer is very much affected by the behaviour of the lender – beware the trap of taking the data at face value.

# 20

## Action-Specific Models
*_by Lois Brown*

### Specific goals and measurable results

Despite massive investment in customer relationship management (CRM) over the past few years, many companies are frustrated with the process and dissatisfied with the results. Yet nobody wants to give up on the objectives of CRM—such as viewing and treating customers as individuals rather than broad segments, managing customer satisfaction proactively rather than reactively, and—let' u not forget—increasing company profits.

In response to this situation, some of the largest financial services companies in North America have augmented their CRM initiatives with predictive modeling software that starts with these specific goals and delivers measurable results. Unlike many software investments, these solutions allow companies to achieve a documented return on their investment in well under a year.

For consumer debt collection, this new generation of predictive modeling software helps meet the goal of improving customer relationships because it predicts how individual customers will react to specific actions. For example, it can help businesses make decisions about which delinquent accounts should be contacted, how they should be contacted (by phone call, email, or letter), and what time of day would be best to reach them by phone.

### Focus resources on productive calls

Following is an example of how predictive modeling can help management make better decisions about how to interact with individual customers. Imagine a credit card customer is several days late with her payment. Normally, you would place a call to this customer (we will call her Mrs. Charles). But what if you could know, before placing the call, that it is likely Mrs. Charles will pay her bill without a collection call. In fact, Mrs. Charles does not mind paying the occasional late fee, but she feels insulted when a collection agent calls her.

Perhaps you have a behavioral scoring system and, under that system, Mrs. Charles has been designated as 'high risk' or 'medium risk' and so goes into collections to be called.

The new generation of predictive modeling ('Action-Specific Modeling'), however, would predict the probability is very high that Mrs. Charles will send in her payment without prompting. Armed with this information, the Collections Manager can be more proactive about managing the company's relationship with Mrs. Charles and remove her from the calling list. The company does not have to spend money on unnecessary calls, and they will not risk offending a valuable customer.

In contrast, a business operating in a reactive mode would not know until Mrs. Charles stopped using her credit card, or even cancelled it, that they may have offended a valuable customer.

Then there is Mr. Williams. A company operating in a reactive mode would not schedule Mr. Williams to receive a collections call because he has been classified by the behavioral scoring system as 'low risk'. The low behavioral score implied he was not expected to become delinquent in the near future. And yet he has missed a payment.

The proactive company using Action-Specific Modeling, however, could predict the probability of Mr. Williams sending in his payment is much higher if he is called. He can then be scheduled for a call, with the knowledge that resources invested in contacting him are necessary to elicit his payment.

**Saves expenses when the decision is "who to call"**
This new predictive modeling technology begins by conducting an experiment (which usually takes a month) and then developing models. These models will predict an outcome based on certain actions. For example, a model could be built to predict the probability of an account making a payment (the outcome) if they are called (action one) or if they receive no call (action two).

This technology is valuable for use with both early-stage and late-stage portfolios. In early-stage delinquencies, the biggest issues are: "Who will pay only if I call?" and "Who will pay no matter what I do?" In early-stage delinquency, 50% or more of those who are delinquent would pay without any collections activity. Identifying those accounts can result in considerable savings in collections resources.

In late-stage delinquencies, the biggest questions are: "Who will never pay no matter what I do?" "Who will pay if my collectors contact them?" And, "Who will pay only when a collection agency contacts them?" This new software can answer all these questions.

Other actions that can be modeled include: low intensity calling versus high intensity calling, letter versus phone call, email versus call, settlement offer versus collection by an agency, and active skip-trace versus letter/no call.

## How the new action-specific modeling technology works

Each action to be tested is applied to a random sample of accounts; the response of those accounts is tracked until sufficient payment data is available. Generally, this takes a month because at least 1,000 accounts must fall into each action and response category (such as action=call and response=payment). Scoring models are developed for each action, using account masterfile (delinquency history, geography, time on file, and balance), relationship information, and possibly a credit bureau report.

Typically, 100 to 250 variables will be considered as potentially explanatory. An automated development process then identifies the 5 to 30 variables that are most predictive of payment.

The specific methodology employed is binary stepwise logistic regression, since this is a proven modeling approach that provides probability estimates in a simple and natural way.

Specifically, the fundamental equation for each account and each action is:

$$\textbf{Prob[Account Cure | Action]} = \exp(\textbf{Score})/[1 + \exp(\textbf{Score})]$$

The key items in this equation are: Prob[Account Cure | Action] = probability account will cure if action is taken and Score = linear combination of explanatory variables, optimized to obtain the best fit of the fundamental equation to the sample. Separate scores are developed for each action.

This new technology continually captures the data that is passed through the system for model rebuilding and reporting. Periodic model rebuilding ensures that the models stay fresh and accurate over time.

**Optimization**

With Action-Specific Modeling it is possible to create an optimized action plan for a group of accounts.

To determine which action should be taken on each account, the traditional rules-based approach would evaluate each account against a set of criteria. This approach becomes very complex with more than two possible choices of action. Rules-based approaches also require human judgment on decisions such as how to determine which calls should be sent to a limited number of agents.

An optimization approach, on the other hand, automatically determines which actions should be taken on which accounts, and takes into consideration all the relevant constraints, so that the amount of money collected is maximized.

The Action-Specific Models consider the impact of actions on individual accounts; optimization then aims to derive the most value from the group as a whole.

**More savings when the decision is "when to call"**

Once Action-Specific Modeling has given management a better picture of just who needs to be called and who does not, it is time to decide when to place the calls that must be made.

Given the high expense of agent resources, the goal is to collect the most money with the resources that are available. This means calling when the right party (the person who can make the promise-to-pay) is most likely to be home to take the call. With perhaps thousands of accounts to call each day, it is important to optimize the overall daily calling schedule. Users of this technology report a 15 % (often greater) increase in right-party contacts.

These results, also, are achieved by optimizing the daily schedule with predictive modeling, together with an integer programming optimization. Scoring models are developed to predict both the best time to call and the probability of getting a promise-to-pay.

The probability of promise-to-pay models are structurally similar to the models mentioned earlier for Action-Specific Modeling. The Best-Time-to-Call models are developed using ternary logistic regression, the fundamental equations of which are:

**Prob[right-party contact | call] = 1/[1 + exp(Score1) + exp(Score2)]**

**Prob[wrong party contact | call] = exp(Score1)/[1 + exp(Score1) + exp(Score2)]**

**Prob[Non-contact | call] = exp(Score2)/[1 + exp(Score1) + exp(Score2)]**

The two scores, Score1 and Score 2, are mutually dependent and developed simultaneously in the modeling process. Separate models of this type are developed for different time periods throughout the day.

"When to call" software captures data from the dialer on the outcome of every call made. Over 150 summary characteristics are generated from the calling history of each account. An example of one such characteristic would be "number of attempts made between 11:00 a.m. and noon on week days over the last 30 days." Models (called scorecards) are developed to predict the probability of getting a right-party contact at each legal calling hour and the probability of getting a promise-to-pay. The predictive models are redeveloped on a regular basis using the historical database, to ensure that they remain current and accurate.

Call targeting strategies can be developed using any available data in the database—such as balance, dollars at risk, and probability of promise-to-pay. Experience and research have shown that, while maximizing right-party contacts alone gives a dramatic improvement versus 'business as usual', adding a 'balance' or 'risk' component can produce substantial increases in money collected. In other words, you call the most right-parties who owe you the most money.

In the daily Call Center production cycle, the "when to call" software picks up a copy of the delinquent account download file (all those accounts which are to be called today). Each account is scored with the appropriate set of scorecards (based on product type, degree of delinquency, and whether the account has been called before). The probabilities of getting a right-party contact, a wrong-party contact, and a non-contact, as well as a promise-to-pay (if a right-party contact is made) are calculated for each account in every time period.

Next, the optimal calling schedule is generated for the day's accounts. This is not as simple as calling each person when he or she is most likely to be home; rather it is fitting in all the calls so that the most money possible is collected over the entire day. This system does not simply tell you to add more resources in order to achieve your goals. Instead, it schedules calls to achieve the highest amount of money collected, given available resources. The methodology used for this optimization is a specialized form of integer programming, which is solved using an adapted version of the simplex method in order to maximize computation efficiency.

Finally, the schedule information is added to each record and the list is sent back to the dialer, which places calls based on the scheduling data. Again, all results are captured for reporting purposes and to continually improve the models.

**How this software affects agent motivation and performance**

Before they began using this new modeling software, many call centers measured list penetration as a surrogate for what they were really trying to improve: talking to more debtors and collecting more money.   But on the 'front lines'—in the call center—focus on the wrong metrics can cause you to reward behavior that does not improve overall collections performance. For example, rewarding personnel for placing and handling the most calls may not effectively increase money collected.   Your operation may focus on number of calls, rather than quality of call results.   Because this new modeling software delivers more right-party contacts, you can reward agents for what they control: their skill at getting promises.

The software can also identify "best practices" among agents at the call center.   For example, reports may show one agent has a shorter talk-time than average but a high promise-to-pay rate. Armed with this information, the supervisor can teach other agents the effective collection tactics being used by the highly productive agent.

Finally, as everyone knows, resource costs and turnover tend to be high in call centers.   Agents report they get more satisfaction from speaking with the right party.   A 15% or 20% improvement in right-party contact rate can have a significant effect on employee satisfaction.

**Benefits are immediate and measurable**

The important goals of CRM often require complex, company-wide initiatives that may take years to fully implement and may never yield easily measurable results.   In the meantime, financial services companies are discovering that predictive modeling software gets immediate results and quick payback.   The business using predictive modeling technology can treat accounts as individuals—not groups—and can manage customer relationships proactively—not reactively.

The improvements in money collected and customer retention begin as soon as the software is implemented. The results can be measured immediately.

Both "who to call" and "when to call" predictive modeling software solutions come with champion/challenger testing features to measure improvement versus business-as-usual and for continual improvement over time. With the champion/challenger feature, it is possible to measure decreases in delinquency roll-rates, decreases in attrition, increases in right-party contacts, increases in promises-to-pay, and other metrics. All of these measurements directly translate to increased profit. For this reason, financial services companies who use this predictive modeling software report payback on their investment in well under a year.

### What to look for in a modeling software provider

Generally it is the larger financial services companies who have led the way in using predictive modeling software to improve business productivity. Therefore you may want to look for a software provider with experience serving the larger banks and credit card companies. Customer service is, of course, critical. The company should be specific about the services it provides, should be prompt and responsive in helping you solve problems, and should have a good reputation. Ask for references and check them.

Because the benefit you derive from the software will be related to the strategies you use, it will be important to choose a provider who has expertise in financial services and collections. The strongest domain expertise comes when the provider's management has had actual, direct experience working in risk and collections at financial services companies. This information may be available on a software provider's web site; check management profiles.

Naturally, the provider must be respected for its use of statistical methods, including logistic regression, and must build models from non-biased samples. Look for a software company that also provides custom modeling, since custom modeling can serve as a research and development test-bed for innovations.

Finally, the point of using this software is to make better business decisions, to increase productivity, and to reduce costs. You want software that provides measurable results and that will give a return on investment in well under a year.

# 21

## Why Scorecards Don't Work
_by Murray Bailey_

### Two types of scorecard

Of course scorecards work. However, the benefits can be harder to achieve than collections would hope and the scorecard developer believes. The reasons for scorecards failing are either poor design of the scorecard or strategy. Let's look at each of these in turn.

A collections scorecard is either general or specific. An example of a general scorecard is 'Collections Entry' - i.e. all accounts entering collections are scored on the scorecard to determine the initial strategy. A specific scorecard is designed for a specific purpose. For example, to determine whether or not to take an action. The design of these two types of scorecard is vastly different and the developer must understand the objective of the scorecard before commencing development. Before we look at specific collections scorecards, let's examine a case study where 'general' was taken to the extreme.

### Don't assume one scorecard is the solution

Order Direct (as we will call them) following the principle of "simplest is best" decided to build a single behavioural scorecard for the whole business. The development was based on taking all existing accounts from the most recent month-end and going back 12 months and selecting those same accounts from that file. Accounts that were written-off or had been defaulted were classed as Bad. Accounts up-to-date or less than 1-cycle in arrears in the recent file were classed as Good. Part of the scorecard is shown in table 21.1.

| Characteristic | Attribute | Point score |
|---|---|---|
| Current Arrears | Up-to-date | 50 |
| | Past due | 30 |
| | Over 30 days | 0 |
| Number of times Past due in the last 3 months | 0 | 30 |
| | 1 | 5 |
| | 2+ | 0 |
| Worst arrears | 0 | 20 |
| | 1 - 2 | 10 |
| | 3+ | 0 |
| Balance declined in past 6 months | Yes | 40 |
| | No | 0 |
| Utilisation | < 50% | 20 |
| | 50% - 69% | 15 |
| | 70% - 84% | 12 |
| | 85% - 99% | 5 |
| | 100%+ | 0 |

Table 21.1 Part of the single behavioural scorecard

The scorecard was applied for authorisations, credit limit increases, shadow limits and early collections. With the new collections system, the scores were also passed into later collections for evaluation.

Eight months after the implementation, an audit of collections discovered that the average write-off per account was approximately 60% higher than a year earlier and it was rising.

The audit identified the primary cause of the increase was authorisations. There was a conflict between the operational rules and the increase strategy. However, even if they had addressed this, there were still major flaws in the scorecard when applied to collections.

Looking at table 21.1, the most powerful characteristic was "Current arrears". All accounts in collections could not score 50 points and so the strength of this characteristic was mainly for authorisations. Similarly for the "Number of times past due in the past 3 months" and "Worst arrears". Customers in collections rarely have declining balances because they are struggling to make payments - so this characteristic is again weaker for collections use.

The "Worst arrears" attributes "1-2" and "3+" were incorrectly assessed for collections risk. Accounts regularly in collections were lower risk than accounts entering and potentially rolling straight to write-off. The fraud issue exacerbated this weakness.

So, Order Direct should have built at least two scorecards and taken very different samples. For the authorisations/credit limit scorecard, the sample should have been of accounts up-to-date or less than 30 days in arrears. The collections scorecard should have been developed on a sample of accounts entering into collections. Better scorecards would have been developed if performance periods and definitions of Bad had been different. A collections scorecard will typically have a performance period of less than six months, whereas a 'sales' based scorecard will be at least 12.

### Specific scorecards
Companies with established collections strategies can make the biggest improvement in performance by building scorecards targeted at a specific action.

The simplest models can provide big business benefits. An example was a scorecard built at Citibank called "the cheques in the post" scorecard. The scorecard was targeted at customers who may have made a payment. Some 80% of card customers who missed their payment paid before 30 days. The objective was to save the expense of the first dunning letter. The scorecard was developed on people that had not paid by the time the letter was due to be sent. The performance period was three days. Anyone paying in the 3 days was 'Good' and therefore already had the cheque in the post. If they paid later, then the letter arguably had an impact and so was justified. By building the specific scorecard the business saved half of the first dunning letter.

Another example of a specific scorecard would be to test the effectiveness of an in-house agency letter, say. The sample selected for development would be accounts that would qualify for the letter (based on arrears and, possibly, a general collections score). The performance period may be 10 days and Good may be defined as a payment received between 4 and 10 days following the posting of the letter. If the objective is to generate contact with the customer, the definition could include an inbound call from the customer followed by a payment within 7 days.

Before you implement a scorecard, check the following:
- What is the objective of the scorecard?
- Was the development sample specific to accounts reaching the point of strategic action?
- What is the outcome period: is it reasonable for the goal?
- What are the definitions of Good and Bad: are they consistent with the strategy and goal?

## Why scorecards fail
If the scorecard was developed with due care, it can still be viewed as failing if the performance does not improve. This can be due to simple reasons, such as poor implementation or objective setting, but it is often due to bad strategy design.

Implementation is a major element of collections scoring. One company developed a general collections score for early collections and decided the first test was to be as a ranking tool in the power dialler. Fundamentally there is a problem with this type of test, however the company set up a champion/challenger environment and plotted cash recovered by the strategies (with and without scoring). After six months there was no significant difference between the strategies. Collections scoring was about to be rejected when a consultant spotted that the power dialler did not have scores in the appropriate field. The main collections system was not passing scores to the power dialler!

The fundamental issue with the test was that the concept was to rank accounts by score rather than the 'value at risk'. The test should have used the score probability (e.g. of rolling to cycle-3) and multiplied this by the balance (or arrears) to measure recoverability and exposure.

**Bad strategies**
Bad strategies usually equate to poorly designed ones. Using decision trees (see chapter 23 for an example) can lead to over complication. I have witnessed letters tested with a day's delay between the champion and challenger and only a handful of accounts reaching the strategy per month.

To be valid, the strategy must be different enough from the champion to provide benefits and have sufficient accounts to produce statistically significant results (see chapter 24 for details on sample size).

Strategies are not 'operational tactics'. A 'December action' where customers were all contacted earlier in the month due to the Christmas holidays is not a strategy unless it is controlled with a group collected in the normal way. Other tactics include switching agents from later telephone collections to pre-delinquent in the last week of the month and door-knocking pre-write-off accounts in the week before they would otherwise roll to write-off at the end of the month.

Other bad strategies may be down to poor design, such as queues that don't match resources or strategies that don't fit with power dialling.

Before you implement a strategy, check the following:
- Is the strategy consistent with the overall objective?
- Is the strategy consistent with the purpose of the scorecard?
- Can the strategy be tracked?
- What performance is expected - for comparison with the results?
- Can you calculate loss (or recovery) impact and cost of collection impact?
- Is the strategy too complicated?
- How long should the test be run for – are there sufficient accounts?
- Could there be an impact on later stages and strategies?
- Do the resources match the strategies?
- Does the test overlap with any other test that might muddy the results?

**The best strategies are a framework**
Scores do not take account of all the information. The history used to develop most scorecards is incomplete. Wherever possible, collections history should be included, but there is always additional information available to the agents.

Inflexible and too slow: this is the criticism often levied at strategies by collections management. They should not be. Collections scoring is about compromise. The scorecard purist will want to run the strategy test for at least the scorecard performance period. However, if it is clearly working (and the collectors will know) then roll it out. The compromise is to maintain a control group so that you can still track the performance against the original strategy.

## Conclusion

Collections scorecards can be extremely effective. However they need to be appropriately designed and executed. Additionally, the scorecard will provide no benefit if it is not used. Optimal collections is about efficiency and this is delivered by having the tools, such as scorecards, to identify the propensity of customers to pay, and the strategies to get the customer to pay.

The best scorecards are those which are designed to address a specific strategic goal within Collections. The best strategies are then the ones that use the risk segmentation and are fine tuned based on a culture of test and learn.

# 22

# Basic Collections Strategies
_by Bayan Dekker_

### Introduction

This chapter examines the application of scoring technology during the delinquency management stage of the credit life cycle. As introduced in an earlier chapter, best practice delinquency management strategies segment accounts according to one of the following account delinquency stages:

- **Early Stage Delinquency** – accounts that have reached a mild state of delinquency, as they missed one or two of the required instalments;
- **Late Stage Delinquency** – accounts which are seriously in arrears, as they have neglected to pay three or more required instalments;
- **Write-off** – accounts with which an organisation will no longer do any future business, as they have been financially written-off and transferred to the profit and loss statement for that financial year.

Once accounts have been correctly segmented and prioritised using the current delinquency state and risk predictors (scores or proxies) determined, the appropriate collections action can be applied.

**Early stage delinquency management**
In this section we will discuss the use of a behaviour risk score in early stage collections, upon accounts that are in early stages of delinquency such as cycle one and cycle 2 delinquent. We will examine possible strategies using behaviour risk scores and profiles.

When managing delinquent accounts, in particular early stage delinquent accounts, it is best practice to use a behaviour risk score to segment accounts into various groups which will receive different treatment within collections. As discussed in a previous chapter, proxies can also be used in the absence of behaviour risk scores.

Correct use of behaviour scores allows an organisation to make best use of collector resources. This is achieved through the allocation of accounts to the correct resources, optimising the timing of actions, and sorting accounts to be worked into the optimum sort-sequence for collection. This allows actions to be delayed on accounts that are likely to cure without collections actions. Any actions taken on these accounts would be wasted resource.

Use of behaviour scores also allows the organisation to maintain good customer service levels where appropriate. One of your organisation's goals is to never make a good customer unhappy. Behaviour risk scores and profiles, if used properly, can prevent embarrassment to the organisation and limit poor customer service.

Balance-at-risk is an important principle in delinquency management. It is calculated by multiplying the risk or recovery propensity of an account (if the score is known) with the outstanding balance on the account. This will quantify the actual balance on an individual account that is likely to go bad or is predicted to reach the bad definition of the scorecard.  Balance-at-risk is an important measure.  If one has a group of early stage delinquent accounts upon which the same action is taken, the best practice sequence in which to work them would be in order of balance-at-risk. One should sort and action the accounts from the highest to the lowest balance-at-risk.

In this illustration of a collections strategy for cycle one delinquent accounts, behaviour risk scores have been grouped into risk profiles.  The Ore profile equates to very low scoring, high risk accounts.  At the other end of the scale, the Diamond profile accounts are very high scoring, low risk.

| Ore | Bronze | Silver | Gold | Platinum | Diamond |
|---|---|---|---|---|---|
| Call after 5 days | | Call after 10 days | | Letter after 10 days | |

Table 22.1 One cycle delinquent accounts

In this example strategy, high risk Ore and Bronze cycle one delinquent accounts receive a collections call five days after billing date. Silver and Gold profiles, which are lower risk 1-cycle accounts, receive a collections call 10 days after billing date. It can be seen that the action has been delayed for the lower risk accounts. These accounts are less likely to go bad than the higher risk accounts on the left and are therefore given more time to pay before being called by the Collections department. Platinum and Diamond profiles, which are the lowest risk cycle one accounts, only receive a collections letter 10 days after billing date. They receive no collections call at this stage. The action of sending a letter is softer than a collections call.  These accounts are the least likely to go bad. They are therefore given time to pay on their own before being reminded to do so by the collections letter.

Self-cure occurs where an account that is delinquent pays to current without any collection action. There should be a high rate of self-cure amongst the lower risk profiles. The rate of self-cures will decrease as the risk increases.

We can now examine the collections strategy for cycle two accounts. Again, behaviour risk scores have been grouped into profiles. The Ore profile equates to very low scoring, high risk accounts. At the other end of the continuum, the Diamond profile equates to very high scoring, low risk accounts.

| Ore | Bronze | Silver | Gold | Platinum | Diamond |
|---|---|---|---|---|---|
| Harsh call at day 0 | | Call after 5 days | | Call after 10 days | |

Table 22.2 Cycle two delinquent accounts

In this example strategy, high-risk Ore and Bronze Cycle two accounts receive a harsh collections call immediately after billing. This is a harsher call than that taken on the Cycle one accounts, reflecting the severity of increased delinquency.

Silver and Gold profiles receive a collections call five days after billing date. Again, this is a harsher call than that taken on Cycle One accounts. This illustrates the concept of 'tilting' of collection actions, which will be explored in more detail in a later section. The action has been delayed for the better risk accounts. These accounts are less likely to go bad than the high risk accounts on the left and are therefore given more time to pay before being followed up by the collections department.

Platinum and Diamond profiles receive their first collections call 10 days after the billing date. Out of all cycle two accounts, these accounts are the least likely to go bad. They are therefore given more time to pay before being called.

**Late stage delinquency management**

We have been discussing early stage collections and the use of behaviour risk scores. In this section we will discuss the use of recovery scores in late stage delinquency management. These accounts have typically reached a delinquency level, which constitutes a 'Bad' account within the behaviour risk scores. The use of a behaviour risk score would be meaningless here, as one would be trying to use a score to predict the likelihood of an outcome that has already occurred.

When managing late stage delinquent accounts, it is best practice to use a recovery score to segment accounts into various groups, which will receive different treatment within collections. Again, proxies can also be used in the absence of recovery scores.

Correct use of recovery scores allows an organisation to make optimum use of internal and external collector resources. This is achieved through the allocation of accounts to the correct resources, optimising the timing of actions, and sorting accounts to be worked into the optimum sort-sequence for collections.

Balance recoverable is an important concept in late stage delinquency management. It is calculated by using the odds of an account repaying its balance (the odds are known if the score is known) and the balance on the account. This will quantify the actual balance on an individual account that is likely to be repaid within a specified period in the future. If one has a group of highly delinquent accounts on which the same action is going to be taken, it is best practice to sequence or order the accounts according to their balance recoverable. One should sort and action the accounts from the highest balance recoverable to the lowest balance recoverable.

Balance recoverable is also important in the handover and write-off decision. If an organisation is considering handing over highly delinquent accounts, those with low balance recoverable should be handed over first. It would not be cost-effective to try to collect on accounts with a low balance recoverable. When determining which accounts to write-off, an organisation should consider writing off low balance recoverable accounts first.

In table 22.3, we are using recovery profiles for accounts that are cycle three delinquent. The low scoring, high risk Ore and Bronze profiles are handed over to an external collections agency according to this strategy. This is because it is not cost-effective to collect on these accounts. Precious internal resources can be allocated to collecting on accounts that will render a higher return. Silver and Gold profiles, which are more likely to repay, receive a letter of demand. This is a harsh action, however the accounts are not handed-over as it is probably cost effective to continue to collect on the accounts internally.

| Ore | Bronze | Silver | Gold | Platinum | Diamond |
|---|---|---|---|---|---|
| Hand-over | | Letter of demand | | Call at 0 days | |

Table 22.3 Cycle three delinquent accounts

Platinum and Diamond profiles, which have the highest likelihood of all cycle three accounts to repay their balance, receive a collections call immediately after billing date. These accounts are the most likely accounts to repay their balances. It is best practice to concentrate collectors on calling on those accounts that will recover the most monies.

| Ore | Bronze | Silver | Gold | Platinum | Diamond |
|---|---|---|---|---|---|
| Write-off | | Hand-over | | Harsh call | |

Figure 22.4 Cycle four delinquent accounts

We are now looking at the collections strategy for cycle four delinquent accounts. Again, recovery scores have been grouped into profiles. Ore and Bronze accounts are written-off. They are highly delinquent and the low recovery score implies that they are not likely to repay their balance. Collecting on these accounts would not be cost-effective.  Silver and Gold profiles are handed over to an external collections agent, as it is more cost-effective to hand these accounts over than to collect on them internally. The action is obviously less harsh than write-off. Platinum and Diamond profiles receive a harsh collections call.  Their recovery profiles indicate that they will repay a significant proportion of their outstanding balances.   However, as they are highly delinquent, they receive harsh actions.

# 23

## Leading Edge Collections Strategies
_by Stephen J Leonard

### Using credit bureau scores
Chapter 18 introduced credit bureau scores. The introduction of credit bureau scores within collections strategies enables increased segmentation but also introduces additional complexities. For example, by utilising both behaviour and credit bureau scores, mismatches in performance can be highlighted.

The interactions of behaviour scores and credit bureau scores within a collections strategy are illustrated in figure 23.1. In this example, accounts are segmented by both scores, which enables finer segmentation of customers than if just the behaviour score is utilised. There will be some customers with Very Low or Low behaviour scores, but Medium to High credit bureau scores. These could be viewed as 'false negatives' in that the customer is under-performing on the organisation's account, but has a good track record on other credit obligations. This may be the result of a customer service dispute and warrants investigation.

Conversely, there are also 'false positives' where the customer appears to be an excellent risk with the organisation, as illustrated by their high behaviour score, but has a poor credit bureau score, which is a result of poor performance on their other credit accounts. This may be an indication that the customer will start to perform in a worse manner with your company in the future.

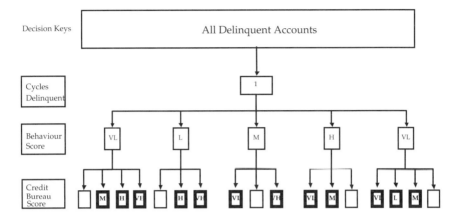

Figure 23.1 Interaction of behaviour score & credit bureau scores

The benefit of the credit bureau score is this form of 'early warning' of poor performance that the individual lender would otherwise be unaware of. In addition there is the opportunity to identify 'true negatives' (customers with Low or Very Low behaviour and credit bureau scores) and 'true positives' (customers with High or Very High behaviour and credit bureau scores).

Whereas the 'true negatives' and 'true positives' support the appropriate decisions within a collections strategy, the question is what can be done operationally with 'false positives' and 'false negatives'?

The solution to these complexities can be found in the calculation of joint odds. Joint odds represent the odds of the customer going 'Bad' based on the observed performance of both the behaviour score and the credit bureau score. As credit bureau scores do not have a fixed score to odds relationship and as it is best practice to re-align behaviour scores on an annual basis, then it is also necessary to calculate the joint odds for an organisation's accounts on an annual basis.

This is a statistical exercise, but the benefit is that the collections manager now has a clear indication of what the odds are for customers, based on their various behaviour and credit bureau scores. Operationally, this means that all accounts can be grouped by their joint odds and then treated appropriately, without concern that there will be a mismatch between risk and the appropriateness of actions taken.

### Using attrition scores

In mature credit markets the cost of attracting new accounts onto a credit grantors books has increased substantially due to heightened competition for new customers and an overall decrease in response rates to credit solicitations and campaigns. Accordingly, this has led to an increased focus on the importance of retaining existing accounts.

An attrition score predicts the likelihood of an account to close or become dormant, thus it is a very powerful tool in an organisations CRM strategy. The collections department of leading edge organisations is increasingly viewed as an important component of any CRM strategy and accordingly, attrition scores are increasingly being utilised within collections strategies.

The logic is that accounts with a low attrition score (i.e. are highly likely to close or become dormant) should be differentiated from those accounts in collections with higher attrition scores. Whereas the concept of 'choose to lose' high risk accounts still prevails, if there are two accounts with a similar acceptable risk and one of these accounts presents a significantly high risk of attrition, then it should receive collections actions that are less harsh than the account with a lower risk of attrition.

This type of strategy is illustrated in figure 23.2. In this example strategy all accounts with a Very Low or Low behaviour score are treated the same regardless of attrition score. However, for accounts with a Medium behaviour score, accounts with a Low attrition score (i.e. have a high likelihood of closure) are treated milder than accounts with a Medium plus attrition score. The same logic is true for accounts with High behaviour scores and Low or Medium plus attrition scores.

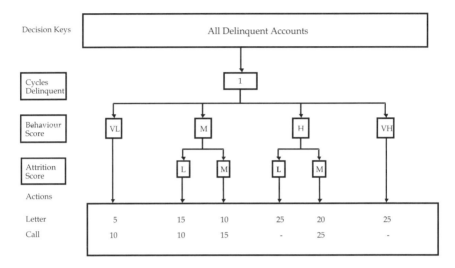

Figure 23.2 Including attrition score in the strategy

These collections strategies, with a CRM focus, have proven to generate positive results in terms of anti-attrition and lower account closure rates, whilst maintaining the same levels of bad debt and write-off.

**Promise to Pay strategies**
One of the most critical elements of any collections strategy is Promise to Pays. However, many companies often overlook the mechanisms around this process, which can then impact collector productivity, collections results and customer service.

An effective collections system requires the functionality to be able to not only set an individual 'Promise to Pay' on an account, but also a series of recurring PTP's.

The collections system needs the ability to automatically convert a PTP into a Broken Promise, after a specified number of days past the promise date have elapsed. Best practice collections systems will also include a PTP payment tolerance parameter.

Best practice PTP follow-up policies include:

- When a customer cannot pay the entire arrears amount required to cure the account to a current status, then it is best practice for the collector to set up a series of recurring PTP's rather than just one PTP for the current month.
- Recurring PTP's increase the collections department's productivity, as the customer does not have to be called each and every month, if they adhere to the agreed payment schedule.
- In addition, there are significant cost-savings as follow-up calls are not required and letter costs can be eliminated.
- For customers sticking to the agreed payment plan, there is also an improvement in customer service, as the collections department does not have to continuously contact them.
- For customers with a single PTP or the first of a series of PTP's, the collections department needs to develop a follow-up PTP strategy.
- Customers can be segmented into three categories: low, medium and high risk. The criteria used to segment the accounts should be behaviour score, but if one is not available, then characteristics such as history of broken promises, returned payments, balance, months on books and level of delinquency should be applied.
- Once the PTP accounts have been segmented into the three risk classes, then different follow-up actions can be applied.
- For high-risk accounts it is best practice to contact the customer with a reminder call on the day before the PTP and also a confirmation call on the day of or the day after the PTP date.
- For medium risk accounts it is best practice to call the customer once. It is worth testing whether it is more

effective to make the reminder call or the confirmation call. The latter call type is more commonly used than a reminder call.

- For low risk accounts it is best practice to drive different follow-up actions by delinquency level and account balance. For low levels of delinquency or low balances at any delinquency level, then low risk customers typically should not get a follow-up confirmation call. For higher delinquency levels or higher balances at any delinquency levels, then it is best practice to set a follow-up confirmation call one to three days after the PTP date.

- For Broken Promises, it is best practice to call these accounts within one day of the PTP converting into a BP. Typically a PTP will convert into a BP 3-5 days from the agreed PTP date.

Strategically, the use of the PTP decision key can be illustrated in figure 23.3.

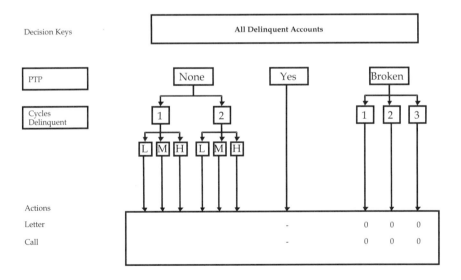

Figure 23.3 Example of the use of the PTP decision key

In figure 23.3, the PTP decision key is used as a high level segmentation tool to group accounts into three main treatment groups: No PTP in effect, PTP in effect, Broken Promise.

Accounts with No PTP in effect are further segmented by behaviour score etc. and the treatment is driven in the standard manner until the account is contacted and hopefully a PTP is made.

Accounts with a PTP in effect are placed in a holding queue until the PTP converts either into a PTP made and the account cures, or the PTP becomes a Broken Promise. The use of this holding queue has a significant positive impact on customer service and also leads to a great reduction in costs, as no letters are generated or calls made.

By utilising the PTP functionality it is no longer necessary to field calls from irate customers who have made a promise, but have still been sent a computer generated collections letter.
Accounts that break a PTP are segmented into Broken Promise queues, which are actioned the day after the promise has been broken. Typically these accounts are sent a Broken Promise letter and also are called as a high priority.

## Tracing strategies
A key component of successful collections strategies is that of tracing, i.e. what to do with accounts with no telephone numbers or return mail.

Tracing is often linked to the data integrity of an organisation and for any company data integrity is a key issue. Unfortunately, in a number of marketplaces, there are a number of challenges impacting data integrity and so tracing is a major component of any collections operation.

Strategically, trace accounts can be segmented using the decision keys illustrated in figure 23.4.

In this strategy Return Post and Missing Telephone decision keys are used as high level segmentation tools to group accounts into four categories.

For 'true trace' accounts, with no standard contact data available, the collections action is to send the accounts directly to the tracing department, or specialist external trace agencies. For accounts with return post but valid telephone numbers, calls are accelerated and letters are not sent. For accounts with valid mailing addresses but no telephone numbers, letters are accelerated. For accounts with valid addresses and telephone numbers, standard account segmentation is used.

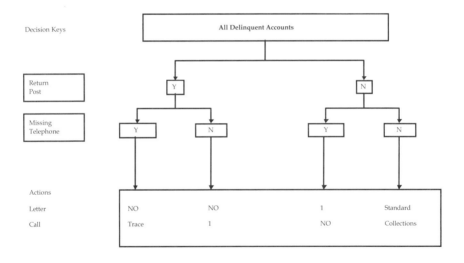

Figure 23.4 Example of Trace account segmentation

The benefits of this form of high-level segmentation are multiple. Accounts that require some form of trace action are identified and actioned immediately, letters are not wasted on return mail addresses, accounts that have no telephone number are excluded from general collections queues or predictive dialler jobs, until they can be rectified. All of these segmentation actions ensure increased collector productivity.

# 24

# Strategy Tracking and Efficiency
_by Murray Bailey_

### Efficiency in Collections

Efficiency in Collections is about matching the appropriate action with the debtor. Taking expensive action too early is inefficient, since many of the customers would have paid without action or with a less expensive action. For example, a credit card company experiences 80% of customers who reach 15 days past due pay by 25 days past due. Taking a blanket action on all these customers such as a telephone call or letter would be inefficient. Overall, volumes are highest in the early stages of arrears and so lower cost actions should be taken. As the customer progresses through the arrears, the likelihood of write-off increases and higher cost action is justified. This assumes that our only method of discriminating by likelihood of write-off is arrears.

Collections scoring provides the lender with the ability to segment the arrears by risk; enabling earlier identification of high-risk accounts against which appropriate higher cost action can be applied. But how do we find the optimum efficiency? To do this we need to measure both drivers of collections cost: write-off and recovery activity. The optimal cost is where the marginal saving in write-off equals the incremental cost of taking an action. This can only be found by testing one set of actions against another for a specific segment of debtors.

The cost of a strategy is total cost of collections plus the cost of the write-offs. However, write-offs can take many months to evaluate. We therefore need a measure that provides a rapid feedback into the evaluation. One such measure is the Collections Efficiency Ratio (CER).

### CER = Probability of write-off + Proportional cost

The proportional cost can be expressed as the cost of collection per account expressed as a ratio of the outstanding balance. In other words the cost of actions for the average balance of a segment of accounts or the cost to collect a pound. If the probability of write-off is the proportion of the balance, we have two ratios that are directly comparable.

If we take the time to write-off as 12 months, the costs must be found for the same accounts over the 'time to write-off'. Typically we use roll rates, however, as long as it is relative, any approximation will do. A word of caution, care must be taken of knock-on effects at later stages if assessment is made prior to actual write-off.

Let us look at an example: Accounts enter Collections and are segmented into strategies. For one strategy, the average balance is £900, the cost of the actions is on average £60. The probability of write-off is 20%. The Proportional cost is 60/900, i.e. 6.7%. The CER is therefore 26.7%. This figure on its own is meaningless. We therefore need to compare it to an alternative strategy to identify the more efficient. A challenger strategy is tested whereby accounts reaching 69 days are telephoned by a Supervisor. The cost of the actions is now on average £70 and the write-off improves to 18%. The challenger CER is 25.8%. Since the challenger CER is lower, this strategy is more efficient. The optimal efficiency is therefore found by continuously testing to find the point at which no more marginal improvement can be found.

## Tracking

Let us say we have four main strategies that are determined by score bands and are applied to accounts selected at 15 days past due. For each strategy we want to test the introduction of a 'consequences' letter at various stages (depending on strategy). It is easy to ignore costs, but if the number of accounts requiring action falls, the cost saving can be significant. Imagine a letter costs £1 and for the low risk group 20% 'self cure' if the letter is delayed by seven days. If there are initially 10,000 accounts we would save 10,000 x 20% x £1 = £2,000 a month.

Table 24.1 shows the champion strategy results and Table 24.2 shows the challenger results. For score band 140 to 169 the challenger is more efficient by 0.5%.

| Scoreband | No. Accts | Ave Bal | Ave Cost | £k w/o | P(w/o) | P(cost) | CER |
|-----------|-----------|---------|----------|--------|--------|---------|-----|
| < 100 | 3987 | 1389 | 80 | 338.1 | 6.1% | 5.8% | 11.9% |
| 100 - 139 | 2110 | 1415 | 78 | 161.4 | 5.4% | 5.5% | 10.9% |
| 140 - 169 | 1879 | 1204 | 66 | 110.1 | 4.9% | 5.5% | 10.3% |
| 170 + | 1255 | 988 | 56 | 31.5 | 2.5% | 5.7% | 8.2% |

Table 24.1 Champion strategy results

| Scoreband | No. Accts | Ave Bal | Ave Cost | £k w/o | P(w/o) | P(cost) | CER |
|-----------|-----------|---------|----------|--------|--------|---------|-----|
| < 100 | 381 | 1391 | 90 | 31.6 | 6.0% | 6.5% | 12.4% |
| 100 - 139 | 219 | 1435 | 84 | 16.4 | 5.2% | 5.9% | 11.1% |
| 140 - 169 | 188 | 1222 | 71 | 9.1 | 4.0% | 5.8% | 9.8% |
| 170 + | 124 | 982 | 60 | 3.5 | 2.9% | 6.1% | 9.0% |

Table 24.2 Challenger strategy results

Behavioural scoring is unlike application scoring in that we have been comparing strategies within score bands. Having determined the more efficient strategy, the score band itself should be tested. Are the cut-offs themselves in the most efficient point? The way to test this is to perform the same analysis, but look at the results either side of the cut-off. The challenger strategy should be tested for debtors in scores higher and lower than the established strategy score band.

Table 24.3 illustrates testing the cut-offs. The existing cut-offs are at 140 and 160. The champion from 130 to 139 is strategy 2. The challenger is strategy 3. From 140 to 159 the challenger is strategy 3. Above 159 the champion is strategy 4 and the challenger is again 3. Comparing the Collections Efficiency Ratios (CER) the appropriate score band for the Strategy 3 is 135 to 159.

| | Champion | | Challenger | |
|---|---|---|---|---|
| Scoreband | Accts | CER | Accts | CER |
| 130 - 134 | 114 | 10.9% | 343 | 10.8% |
| 135 - 139 | 188 | 10.3% | 532 | 10.7% |
| 140 - 144 | 345 | 9.9% | - | |
| 145 - 149 | 654 | 9.5% | - | |
| 150 - 154 | 521 | 9.1% | - | |
| 155 - 159 | 489 | 9.1% | - | |
| 160 - 164 | 105 | 8.9% | 417 | 8.5% |
| 165 - 169 | 98 | 8.8% | 392 | 8.3% |

Table 24.3 Challenging the score band

## Case study and significance

A large US credit card company (we will call them Cardbank) tested a Collections Entry strategy, varying the timing of the first outbound telephone call. There were two challengers each comprising 10% of accounts entering Collections. Challenger 1 was to telephone later, while the challenger 2 strategy was to telephone earlier. 70,000 accounts were up to date and missed the payment date. Of these, 58% paid before five days past due. 70% of 60 day accounts rolled to write-off.

Table 24.4 shows the roll rates to 60 days past due. To calculate ultimate loss Cardbank assumed the performance after 60 days was independent of the first call. So rather than calculate the ultimate write-offs, Cardbank used the relative difference between the roll rates. The cost per account also provides a relative measure that we can use to calculate the CER. Table 24.5 shows the CER calculation to 60 days past due. The roll rate from table 24.4 is the relative Probability of write-off, P(w/o) and the Proportional cost, P(cost) is the average cost per account divided by the average balance per account ($2,000).

| Strategy | Accounts Entering | Roll 5 to 60 | Cost per acct |
|---|---|---|---|
| Champion | 56,000 | 4.55% | $5.24 |
| Challenger 1 | 7,000 | 4.62% | $4.59 |
| Challenger 2 | 7,000 | 4.41% | $5.62 |

Table 24.4 Strategy comparison

Strategy 2 had the lower roll rate, but higher cost due to telephoning a greater number of customers. However, the CER, considering both the cost and roll rate, was lowest for this strategy and so Cardbank implemented the earlier call shortly thereafter.

| Strategy | P(w/o) | P(cost) | CER |
|---|---|---|---|
| Champion | 4.55% | 0.26% | 5.81% |
| Challenger 1 | 4.62% | 0.23% | 4.85% |
| Challenger 2 | 4.41% | 0.28% | 4.69% |

Table 24.5 CER comparison by strategy

With a sample size = n and Roll rate = R, you can expect that 95 times out of 100, the subsequent roll rate will be in the range

$$R \pm 1.96 \times \sqrt{(R \times (100 - R)/ n )}$$

In the case study, we had a sample size of 7,000 reduced to 5,950 (n) for each Challenger since 15% of accounts entering Collections pay before five days past due. The roll rate (R) is 4.55%. We should therefore expect that a subsequent roll rate will be in the range.

$$4.55\% \pm 1.96 \times \sqrt{(4.55\% \times 95.45\% / 5,950)}$$

equals $4.55\% \pm 0.53\%$, (at the 95% confidence level).

Therefore neither challenger was significantly different from the champion at this level of confidence. A significant challenger roll rate would have to have been better than 4% to have justified implementation.

Is it right to use the 95% confidence level? If you were 50% sure, half of the time you would expect to be wrong. This is unlikely to be acceptable, however the degree of confidence really depends on the appetite for risk that the business wishes to take. A more reasonable way of improving the certainty of the test is to increase the sample size. Either test a larger number of cases, or run it for a period of months.

We know roughly what roll rate to expect (R). If we do not want the error to be more than E%, then the sample size should be more than:

$$n = R \times (100 - R) \times (1.96 / E)^2$$

If Cardbank were looking for a 0.2% benefit in roll rates, then the error (E) should be less than 0.2%. The sample size should therefore be at least:

$$n = 4.55\% \times 95.45\% \times (1.96 / 0.2\%)^2 = 41,710$$

or seven months using the 10% test group.

**Think before you leap**

In conclusion, the design of your test is just as important as coming up with an idea for a new strategy. When you plan your test you must think about the following:

- What degree of improvement do you need to see?
- How confident does the business expect you to be with your predicted result?
- How will you measure ultimate losses?

Key to all of these is sample size. If there are insufficient numbers of accounts, reconsider your sample selection or plan that the sample will be over a range of months. In Collections we want immediate results, sometimes we need the discipline of patience to wait for our results to be meaningful.

# 25

## Customer Centric Collections and Scoring
_by Murray Bailey

### Customer rather than account

Banks and some large lenders have customers who have multiple products. It can therefore be frustrating to both the customer and the Collections team to find that there are multiple contacts when the customer is in arrears. The concept of customer centric collections is by no means new and yet many organisations are still a long way from achieving this objective.

The issues are primarily around the systems and organisation, although the complexity of handling the payment is an additional problem. Legacy systems tend to be vertical, delivering functionality specific to the requirements of the product. Whilst the fundamentals of collections activity are the same, each product has its nuances. For example Mortgage collections systems tend to be simpler with more focus on individual treatment and re-establishment of bank payments whereas a small revolving facility will rely on a high degree of automation and clever segmentation to identify the most effective early action, channelling accounts into the dialler only when the probability of payment following a letter falls below a certain level.

Modern systems allow for strategies to be segmented at product level and can even be set based on combinations of products. Middleware is also available so that the benefits of a customer view can be achieved without the need to replace legacy systems, thus saving time and money.

The organisational issue is also a temporary hurdle. If the business is willing to move to a customer view, rather than operate in silos, then the culture will be ready for change. However, if the business is not ready, you will find the politics will block your efforts. The willingness must come from the top and successful companies have found that the gradual progression towards a customer centric solution works best. Even before systems are compatible, staff can be cross trained and share goals. And when systems are available, the migration may be one product at a time. This provides the operation with the ability to learn and tune the system on lower risk portfolios before attempting to link in more complex systems.

**Pros and Cons**
Let's deal with the downside first since there is only one. It is complexity. It would be nice to make a single customer contact and obtain a single payment that could be assigned to the products automatically. However this is no simple calculation for this assignment. In addition there is no simple risk assessment of customers with multiple products. How do you view the long term customer with a large mortgage that is in order, but is two months in arrears on his credit card in comparison to the customer who is paying the minimum on his up-to-date credit card, but misses his mortgage instalment. We will look at the issue of combining risk assessment later. For now we will consider the upsides.

Some organisations start down the customer centric road with the motivation of reducing overheads. Having a single team provides economies of scale. In addition there are the benefits of flexibility –

larger numbers of staff mean that deployment to areas requiring attention doesn't necessarily mean that another area will suffer. Cross training and staff development and progression are also benefits associated with a larger combined team.

There will be customer relationship benefits associated with the one-call approach. In addition, the reduced contacts will result in lower collections costs as letters and calls are combined. However these financial benefits pale in comparison to the opportunity to reduce write-offs. A rigorously executed customer centric strategy can deliver large improvements to the bottom line. By a better assessment of the customer risk and probability of loss, companies have seen write-offs reduce by up to 25%.

## Approaches

So how is it done? The biggest mistake that companies make is to try and do too much too quickly. The key to success is to ensure that the three key elements are ready: the people, the systems and the strategies. The best companies see the development of customer centricity as a progression.

There are three stages of the development of customer centric collections. The most simple is to provide a flag to the agent so that when they are working an account they can see that there is another product. However access to the detail of the other product is manually intensive, requiring a 'hot-key' between systems.

The second stage continues with an informative approach rather than one that is data driven. Here the agent is provided with the other product details without the need to hot key. This approach may commence with silos, but addresses the ability of the agent to more easily enter into a discussion about the customer's complete relationship with the bank. The progression of the solution is therefore to enable the agent to take actions that can be applied to all of the range of products rather than the single account.

There is a third approach is to consider the holistic position of the customer and design the collection strategy at the customer level. To achieve this solution, the organisation must have mechanisms and models in place to assess the customer so that the strategy can be determined at the customer level.

### Customer assessment

In the late 1990s a major UK bank developed customer level scores for use in Collections. The implementation coincided with a new customer centric system. The concept was that any collector could work any account and since a high proportion of customers had multiple accounts one call could resolve a number of collections issues. In addition the collections score would depend on all products and so enable a better assessment of the customer's willingness and ability to pay.

Within a matter of months collections returned to silos. What had happened is that mortgage accounts were being collected on whereas the credit card portfolio deteriorated rapidly. The problem was explained as one of prioritisation. The high balances on the mortgages dominated both the prioritisation and the productivity. The group risk manager said "It was a wake up call to the Collections risk team. The theory was great, but practically the initial solution didn't work."

A business with a high proportion of customers holding multiple products may be in a position to build scorecards that reflect those multiple product holdings. Such models are be more predictive than account based models, but care must be taken to ensure definitions are appropriate and samples truly reflect product holdings. For example a bank with overdrafts and credit cards are likely to require a model for customers with overdrafts alone, a model for credit card customers and a third for dual product holding.

The alternative to customer scoring is to combine account scores. The combination depends on the weighting of risk by product and relies on the alignment of scores so that each product is appropriately assessed in combination.

Figure 25.1 illustrates a solution to customer scoring where a product dominates. The dotted lines reflect 'no risk' inputs. Transaction information may influence the score, but the payment information is not predictive. However, there will be customers who do not have an overdraft or do not pay the other products. These customers will have a customer score that is dependent on the payment performance of the accounts. This second scenario is therefore a separate customer score.

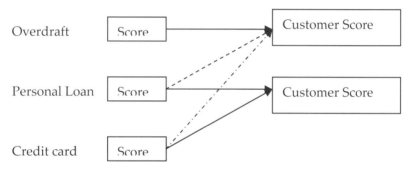

Figure 25.1 Combining risks to form a customer level risk

**Conclusion**
The most advanced, customer centric collections is not appropriate for every company. Simple solutions, such as providing hot-key data to agents can work well where multiple product holding is not a high proportion of the business. However where there are multiple products, and especially where a current account relationship exists, the benefits of customer centric collections are enormous.

The ideal solution is complicated and the recommendation is to progress in stages towards a goal of fully integrated customer systems and strategies. There is a learning cycle where systems must be designed and models built to appropriately assess the combined probability of write-off.

# GLOSSARY OF TERMS

**Abandon Rate -** A measure of customer service quality based on the percentage of total incoming calls to a customer service center that are abandoned by customers because they are placed on hold too long.

**Abandoned Call -** The caller hangs up before reaching the agent. Also called a lost call.

**Absolute Priority Rule (APR) -** The order of payment used in many bankruptcy litigation systems. Typically, major creditors are fully compensated before minor creditors receive anything, and minor creditors are fully compensated before shareholders receive anything.

**ACD -** Acronym for Automatic Call Distributor. It is used in call centres for routing calls to available agents, holds overflow calls, gives and takes messages and provides reports. See also Automatic Call Distributor

**ACH -** The process whereby incoming calls are answered and handled by a pre-recorded script, using specialist computer and telecoms equipment. See also Automated Call Handling, IVR, VIC

**Adaptive Control System -** A computer system that automates and manages the ongoing risk management function of accounts. It typically includes behaviour scoring, champion-challenger strategies, decision keys and reporting. It may be run on a mainframe or on personal computers, either singly or networked.

**Adverse Action Notice -** A lender's notice to refuse, end, or reduce credit. Under the U.S. Fair Credit Billing Act, creditors must disclose the reason.

**Agent -** The person who handles incoming or outgoing calls. Also referred to as a customer service representative (CSR), telephone sales or telephone service representative (TSR), rep, associate, consultant, engineer, operator, technician, account executive, team member, customer service.

**Agent Group** - Also called Split, Gate, Queue or Skills Group. A collection of agents that share a common set of skills, such as being able to handle customer complaints.

**Agent Out Call** - An outbound call placed by an agent.

**Agent Status** - The mode an agent is in (Talk Time, After-Call Work, Unavailable, etc.).

**Answer Call - A** call counted as answered when it reaches an agent (when referring to an agent group).

**Automatic Call Distributor (ACD)-** This is used in call centres for routing calls to available agents, holding overflow calls, giving and taking messages and generating reports.

**Auxiliary Work State -** An agent work state that is typically not associated with handling telephone calls. When agents are in auxiliary mode, they will not receive inbound calls.

**Available State -** Agents who are signed on to the ACD and waiting for calls to arrive.

**Available Time -** The total time that an agent or agent group is waiting for calls to arrive, for a given time period.

**Average Handle Time (AHT) -** The sum of Average Talk Time and Average After-Call Work for a specified time period.

**Average Time to Abandonment -** The average time that callers wait in a queue before abandoning. The calculation considers only calls that are abandoned.

**Bad Rate -** The percentage of accounts performing in an unsatisfactory manner, as determined by the good/bad definition used at the time the scorecard was developed.

**Bads -** Accounts that the credit grantor wishes they had not accepted. In Collections scoring terms, typically someone who has not paid (enough) during the performance period.

**Balance -** The amount of funds outstanding on an account.

**Balance At Risk (BAR) -** The value that is calculated by multiplying the accounts balance by the probability that it will go bad.

**Balloon Payment -** A final lump-sum payment that includes remaining unpaid principal. The extra payment extinguishes the debt.

**Bankruptcy -** The legal process by which a consumer or business declares insolvency.

**Base Staff -** The minimum number of agents required to achieve service level and response time objectives for a given period of time. Seated agent calculations assume that agents will be in their seats for the entire period of time. Therefore, schedules need to add in extra people to accommodate breaks, absenteeism and other factors that will keep agents from the phones. Also called Seated Agents.

**Behavioural Scoring -** A scoring system for assessing the performance of an existing account. Scores are typically risk-based but can be applied to any performance objective. Also known as Behaviour Scoring and Performance Scoring.

**Bench Marking -** The process of comparing measurements or indexes relative to on another, allowing the identification of 'best practice' methods and measurements.

**Benchmarking Consortium -** An industry group that seeks to set benchmarks of best practice or performance for a given industry or sector.

**Block Code -** A code used by credit grantors to identify specific accounts and typically block them from taking additional credit.

**Call Abandonment -** This refers to people, who when placed on hold at an incoming call centre, elect to 'abandon' the call. Call centres monitor the 'abandonment rate' very closely, as it is a predictive measure of their efficiency. See also abandonment.

**Call Blending** - Combining traditionally separate inbound and outbound agent groups into one group of agents responsible for handling both inbound and outbound mode and outbound contacts. A system that is capable of call blending automatically puts agents who are making outbound calls into the inbound mode and vice versa, as necessitated by the incoming call load.

**Call by Call Routing** - The process of routing each call to the optimum destination according to real-time conditions.

**Call Centre** - An umbrella term that generally refers to reservations centres, help desks, information lines or customer service centres, regardless of how they are organised or what types of transactions they handle. Many are challenging the term, because calls are just one type of transaction and the word center doesn't accurately depict the many multi-site environments.

**Call Control Variables** - The set of criteria the ACD uses to process calls. Examples including routing criteria overflow parameters, recorded announcements and timing thresholds.

**Call Detail Recording** - Data on each call, captured by the ACD. This can include the trunk used, time in queue, call duration, agent who handled the call, number dialed (for outgoing) and other information.

**Call Tracking** - Keeping track of what happened to customer calls.

**Can't Pays** - Debtors who have defaulted on payments due to their financial inability rather than any intent not to pay.

**CHAID** - Acronym for Chi Square Automatic Interaction Detection.

**Challenger Strategy** - A proposed strategy as an alternative to the existing 'Champion' strategy.

**Champion Strategy** - The existing strategy in use by the credit grantor.

**Champion-Challenger Test** - The process of testing the Challenger strategy against the incumbent Champion strategy, using statistically valid testing and control groups of accounts.

**Characteristic** - A question asked on an application or an item of information on a credit report. For example, Age, Occupation, Marital Status. For behaviour scoring models, the characteristics are generated from payment and purchase information, such as Delinquency Level, Utilisation, and Months Since Last Active.

**Characteristic Analysis** - A comparison of the statistical distribution of counts or percentages of the attributes of characteristics in the current applicant population with those in the sample that was used to develop the original system.

**Cohort** - A group of items sharing a common quality, for example all accounts that were opened in the same month. Also known as a Tranche.

**Coincident Flow Rates** - The product of the individual net flows from current to write-off for a given two-month period. Changes in the flow rates provide a measure of the overall efficiency of the collections department.

**Collateral** - Assets set aside and pledged to a lender for the duration of a loan. If the borrower fails to meet the loan obligations, the lender has a claim to these assets.

**Collection** - An account in default for which the creditor attempts to receive payment. Indicates any account/trade that reflects a collection status, special comment, narrative, remarks, or collection segment ID.

**Collections Scorecard** - A statistically derived behavioural scorecard developed for predicting the future risk of accounts in the early stages of collections.

**Compound Flows** - The percentage of the balances that are current, which will eventually be written-off. This is a method of making reserves or provisions for write-off.

**Computer Telephony Integration (CTI)** - The software, hardware and programming necessary to integrate the computer and telephone so that they can work together seamlessly and intelligently.

**Contractual Delinquency** - The level of an accounts delinquency calculated by the total number of months of outstanding payments due.

**Contractually Liable** - Those parties who are expressly obligated to repay all debts arising on an account by reason of an agreement to that effect.

**Credit Bureau Report** - The information resulting from an enquiry to a Credit Bureau. At minimum this will be judgments or enquiry volumes. Many countries Credit Bureau also provide data on current and previous loans and accounts.

**Credit Reference Information** - The information resulting from an enquiry to a credit bureau's database.

**Cycles Delinquent** - The number of billing cycles that an account has failed to make a qualifying payment for. For example 2 cycles delinquent means that an account has missed 2 qualifying payments. See also Dunning Level.

**Database Call Handling** - A system whereby the ACD works in synchronisation with the database computer to process calls, based on information in the database. For example, a caller inputs digits into a voice processing system; the database retrieves information on that customer and then issues instructions to the ACD on how to handle the call (e.g. where to route the call, what priority the call should be given in the queue, the announcements to play, etc.).

**Day of Week Routing** - A network service that routes calls to alternate locations, based on the day of the week. There are also options for day of year and time of day routing.

**Debt Service** -The schedule for the repayment of interest and principal amount on an outstanding debt.

**Decision Tree** - A tree-shaped graphical representation of the relationships between a dependent variable and a set of independent variables. Typically, the dependent variable is positioned at the top or left of the tree (root node), while independent variables (nodes) and their relationships are shown as branches in the tree. Also called a classification tree.

**Deed of Settlement -** The written record of the final resolution of an action or dispute between the parties. A deed of settlement may be made by an order of the court.

**Default Judgment -** Judgment granted to the Plaintiff in the absence of and without hearing the defendant. This judgment is taken when the defendant fails to indicate to the court that he wishes to defend the action, fails to plead or fails to attend the trial.

**Default Notice -** A notice that must be sent to customers who are in arrears, before litigation or other recovery actions can be taken to recover the debt. Once the notice has been served, the lender has the right to demand repayment of the full balance outstanding rather than only the arrears or over limit amount outstanding.

**Default Probability -** The likelihood of default on a debt within a stated timeframe.

**Delinquency -** Failure to make a loan payment on time. Delinquent loans payments may be subject to a late fee, expressed as a flat fee or a percentage of the amount due.

**Delinquent -** A rating assigned to accounts when the consumer fails to make the obligatory payments. An account is delinquent when the credit obligations (payments) are not meeting the current definition (for example, an account that is 30 days delinquent has missed one month of payments; an account that is 60 days delinquent has missed two months of payment; etc.).

**Derogatory -** A rating assigned to accounts when the consumer fails to make the obligatory payments and is turned over for special handling, such as collections, charge-off, repossession, etc.

**Divergence -** A measure of the strength of the scorecards. This is the distance between the means of the score distributions of Good and Bad accounts or applications. The greater the divergence, the better.

**Dunning Letter -** A collections letter that is sent to a delinquent account in order to elicit payment.

**Dunning Level -** The number of billing cycles that an account has failed to make a qualifying payment for. For example dunning level 2 means that an account has missed 2 qualifying payments. See also Cycles Delinquent.

**Dynamic Answer -** An ACD feature that automatically reconfigures the number of rings before the system answers calls, based on real-time queue information. AS costs do not commence until the ACD answers calls, this feature can save callers or the call center money when long distance charges apply.

**Dynamic Delinquency Report -** A report that is produced monthly or quarterly to monitor the growth in the delinquency levels for a set of accounts, which have been open for approximately the same length of time. Also known as a Dynamic **Performance Cohort Matrix or Vintage Analysis.**

**Efficient Collectables -** A classification of accounts that identifies account holders who will respond to collections activity.

**Full Payers -** Credit cardholders who pay their balance off in full each month, thereby incurring no interest. As called Transactors.

**Gini Coefficient -** A statistical measure of the efficiency of a scorecard.

**Good -** An applicant that the business would elect to underwrite, given the benefit of hindsight. In Collections terms, a Good is typically one who pays within the performance period.

**Good/Bad Odds -** The likelihood that an applicant or an account will perform in a satisfactory manner. For example 10 to 1 means that out of 11 applicants or accounts, 10 will perform well and one will not.

**Good/Bad Definition -** The precise business definition of good and bad accounts. This also includes definitions of indeterminate accounts and exclusions.

**Guarantor -** A guarantor undertakes to pay debts incurred by a third party. The guarantor is liable for any shortfall or default on the borrower's debt.

**Information Odds -** The statistical odds that an applicant will become a good risk. It is calculated from the information known about the applicant.

**Insolvent -** One who is unable to meet or pay his liabilities and who in consequence has surrendered his estate for the benefit of his creditors or whose estate has been compulsorily sequestrated by a creditor/creditors.

**Instalment -** An account relationship where the credit obligation and the payment amounts are established for a fixed period of time. Set payments are made at agreed intervals until the debt is fulfilled.

**Intelligent Agents -** Computer programs able to act independently based on limited decision-making capabilities.

**Interactive Voice Response (IVR) -** This is equipment connected with an ACD that permits inbound callers to a call centre to choose their own routing of the call.

**Interval Bad Rate -** The proportion of the overall population that is 'bad' for a given score.

**Interval Statistics -** A table of scoring results that shows the percentage of accounts that can be expected to achieve any particular score.

**Judgment -** An obligation (or debt) created by the decree of a court.

**Judgment Debt -** A sum payable under a judgment or order enforceable by a court.

**Lagged Flow Rates -** The product of net flows whereby the flows are taken from the same tranche of balances. Thus if the net flow from January to February is used for the current to 1-cycle flow, then the months of February to March will be used for the 1-cycle to 2-cycle flow.

**Letter of Demand -** An initial document indicating the Plaintiff's claim and the consequences if the Defendant does not comply with his request.

**Liability -** A legal obligation or duty, an amount owed.

**Lien -** A charge upon real or personal property for the satisfaction of some debt or duty ordinarily arising by operation of law. (2) A creditor's claim on a debtor's collateral.

**MIS -** Abbreviation for 'Management Information System.'

**Node -** A location defined by branch attributes on a tree. The root node is the initial node and all branches originate from it. The nodes on the bottom-most branches of the tree are the terminal nodes or leaves.

**Non-regular Payments** - These are payments made on an irregular basis, payment amounts also tend to vary. Typically, customers with irregular income such as farmers would make use this type of payment scheme.

**Non-Sufficient Funds (NSF) -** The returned payment reason code for when a customer's cheque payment is returned for lack of funds in their current account.

**Normal Distribution -** A function that represents the distribution of many random variables as a symmetrical bell-shaped graph. Also known as Bell Curve and Gaussian Distribution.

**Odds -** The statistical probability of a positive outcome arising from any financial risk. For example, a good account from a home loan, or minimal claims on an insurance policy.

**Outcome Period -** The period between the application window and the good/bad definition being set.

**Outsourcing -** The process of having various database functions handled by external service bureaus.

**Overall Odds -** The product of the Information Odds and the Population Odds. Also known as Total Odds.

**Performance Definition -** The definition of what constitutes Good, Bad and Indeterminate accounts.

**Performance Period -** The period of time for which the Performance Definition is applicable. For example, in Behaviour Scoring, the performance period is typically 6 months.

**Performance Scoring -** A scoring system used to estimate the probability that an existing account will go bad. It is developed using account behaviour data, such as payment and purchase activity and is typically calculated on a monthly basis. Also known as Behavioural Scoring.

**Portfolio Bad Rate -** The overall bad rate for the portfolio above, and including, a specific score. The overall portfolio bad rate is that of the lowest score.

**Positive Shift -** A movement in the population towards a lower risk portfolio.

**Power Dialling** software – A system that automatically dials telephone numbers in volume, and presents 'connects' to a team of agents

**Pre-dialling** software is resident on each agent's PC and automatically dials a highlighted number when the collector hits a function key.

**Predictive Dialling Software – An** automatic dialling system that predicts, on the basis of recent past performance, how long the call will last. The dialling is then paced to match agent resources.

**Principal** - The amount of a loan, excluding interest, or the amount invested, excluding income.

**Recency Delinquency -** A measurement of delinquency, whereby an accounts delinquency status is governed by the last time it made a qualifying payment.

**Recoveries -** The amount of funds that are collected from accounts that have been previously charged-off.

**Regression Analysis -** A statistical method using formulae to combine the information from known variables to predict an unknown variable, i.e. using characteristics to predict risk.

**Rescission -** A court order setting aside a default judgment.

**Risk -** The statistical likelihood of an account becoming a bad risk in the future. Risk is measured in odds or percentages.

**Risk-Based Pricing -** A strategy in which the interest rate or other terms and conditions are driven by the perceived risk of the account or customer.

**Risk-Reward Trade-off -** This is the trade-off or calculation that an organisation makes when setting the cut-off score for accepting applicants. Higher risk applicants will tend to generate higher rewards and lower risk applicants will tend to generate lower rewards

**Roll Rate -** The percentage of accounts or balances rolling forward from one level of delinquency to the next level of delinquency.

**Roll Rate Analysis -** Analysis showing the percentage of accounts that move from one level of delinquency into worse levels. Conversely, there are also accounts that reduce their levels of delinquency.

**Root Node -** The node at the very top of a hierarchical tree display. This node also represents the overall distribution of values of the dependent variable.

**Rule Induction -** The extraction of useful if/then rules from data that is based on statistical significance, for explanatory or predictive purposes.

**Rule Set -** A binary formula that determines processing. A rule set can be a step in an execution path.

**Satisfactory Accounts -** Accounts that perform according to the terms and conditions of account usage, as defined by the credit grantor. Also known as Goods.

**Score -** The total number of points that an application accrues by summing all of the weightings corresponding to the answers given on the application form and relevant data retrieved from internal or external data sources.

**Score Band -** A narrow range of scores that are grouped together to form a statistically meaningful unit. These are used for monitoring purposes. Also known as Score Interval.

**Score Distributions -** The distributions of the Good scores and the Bad scores.

**Score Misalignment Report -** A report detailing by attribute how even the nature of the score/ odds relationship is. Where the relationship is not even, the scorecard may require re-weighting.

**Score to Odds Relationship -** The relationship between the score and the odds. For example a behaviour score of 660 may have associated odds of 15 Goods to 1 Bad.

**Scorecard -** A table listing the characteristics that provide the most predictive information and the attributes and weightings associated with each characteristic.

**Scorecard Power -** There are a number of statistical measures for quantifying the potential strength of a scorecard. These include R-squared, information value, coefficient of determination, exchange coefficient, divergence and the Kolmogorov-Smirnoff statistic.

**Segmentation -** The act of breaking up a set of field values into discrete groups based on similarity. Clustering and classification trees are methods of segmenting data without or with a dependent, respectively.

**Segmentation Analysis -** The process of determining how to effectively split the total population into sub-populations, in order to develop separate scorecards for the sub-populations.

**Self-cures -** A classification of accounts used with Collections Triage(tm) that identifies account holders that will cure the delinquency, before being three cycles delinquent, without or with little collections activity.

**Settlement -** The reporting and transfer of settlement amounts owed by one institution to another, as a result of clearing.

**Short settlement -** An agreed amount, which is less than the full amount due, that the debtor will pay, and the creditor will accept, in full repayment of the debt.

**Smooth Call Arrival -** Calls that arrive evenly across a period of time. This is virtually non-existent in incoming call environments.

**Split -** A division of a data set based on the values found in a single field (or function of fields). Used to determine the number of scorecards required to describe the data.

**Statement Message -** A text message that appears on a customer's statement. This is often used for marketing or delinquent collections purposes.

**Straight Rollers -** A classification of accounts that identifies account holders who will charge-off or declare bankruptcy within a specific period of their initial delinquent event, regardless of collections activity.

**Strategy Management Systems -** Proprietary systems for implementing account management strategy design and testing for application or behavioural scoring.

**Sub-population -** Any sub-group, within the main population, that is sufficiently and significantly different from the rest of the population, to warrant being monitored, evaluated or potentially scored separately.

**Subpoena -** A summons issued by the court calling upon a person to attend the court on a certain day, at a time specified, for the purpose of giving evidence in a certain case, under a penalty in the event of failure to do so.

**Suit -** An action or process in a court for the recovery of a right or claim.

**Sum-of-Cycle Report -** A report that is produced at cycle billing, rather than at month-end.

**Testator -** Person appointed to execute a valid will.

**Total Odds -** The product of the Information Odds and the Population Odds. Also known as Overall Odds.

**Trace -**An operational function dedicated to finding debtors who have absconded without leaving a forwarding address or contact point.

**Tranche -** A group of accounts opened in the same time period. Alternatively known as a Cohort.

**Transactors -** Card account-holders who pay off their balance in full each month.

**Transition Matrix -** Gives the likelihood of an account, in any one state at one point in time, moving into any other state at a second point in time.

**Unexpected Losses** - A common term used to describe exceptionally large losses.

**Universal Agent -** Refers to either an agent who can handle all types of incoming calls or an agent who can handle both inbound and outbound calls.

**Unsatisfactory Accounts -** Accounts that have not performed according to the terms and conditions specified by the credit grantor. Also known as Bads.

**Up Selling** - A technique for prompting customers to buy upgraded or premium products.

**Update -** The process of modifying or inserting new information onto a stored record. Updating can be done either in an on-line environment or via batch method.

**Upper-bound -**In a decision tree, the manner in which an input value, (which comes from the application processing system or account management system), is compared with the value of a decision key. An upper bound comparison means that a match occurs if the input value is less than or equal to the key value.

**Validation -** The process of testing the final scorecard before delivery. This is undertaken by the supplier and the process should be repeated by the user prior to the scorecard being implemented in a live environment.

**Validation Sample -** A small percentage of the development sample, (typically 20%), that is excluded from the scoring model development, so that it can be used to test the statistical validity of the final scorecard. Also known as Hold-out Sample.

**Variable -** A column in a database that contains the same kind of information for each record. For example, an Age field contains the age of each person in the database. A variable can be either dependent or independent. Also known as Attribute and Field.

**Virtual Call Center -** A distributed call center that acts as a single site for call handling and reporting purposes.

**Voters Roll (VR) -** The electoral register.

**WATS -** Acronym for Wide Area Telephone Service. This is typically a call free of charge for the person initiating the call.

**Weight of Evidence -** A quality index for a piece of information that indicates the strength of the information towards explaining the difference in the level of some binary outcome variable.

**Weightings -** The values that correspond to each attribute in a scorecard. Also referred to as Weights or Point Scores.

**Won't Pays -** Debtors who have defaulted on payments and deliberately choose not to pay for whatever reason. They usually have the ability to pay but not the intent.

**Workforce Management Software -** A software system that forecasts call loads, calculates staff requirements, organises schedules and tracks real-time performance of individuals and groups.

**Write-off -** A lender's declaration of a balance as uncollectable bad debt and/or the process of writing off uncollected loans from account receivable books.

**X-Days -** A credit card industry term to describe accounts that are between 1-29 days delinquent. Also known as 1-Cycle accounts.

**Young Accounts -** Refers to accounts that are too new to have enough payment and spend data to utilise a behaviour score. The typical definition of young accounts lies within the range of 1-6 months.

# ABOUT THE AUTHORS

**Murray Bailey**

Murray Bailey started in risk management in 1985 after a career with Coopers & Lybrand. He has held senior roles at GE Capital, Citibank, Household International, Welbeck Finance and is currently Managing Director at Windsor. He has managed collections and collection agency operations both directly and indirectly and been responsible for collections scorecards and strategies. Murray obtained a first class BSc in Physics and passed the Maths Part III Tripos at Cambridge University. Murray is a regular conference speaker, a credit trainer, and specialises as a consultant in credit quality matters for the consumer credit industry.

**John Berkin**

John Berkin is a Director of City Consulting Associates, with industry expertise in telecoms, banking and finance. His specialisation over the last ten years has been mass-market finance and lending in the UK and Europe. He has worked with three other consultancy and IT organisations: AMS (MD – UK), Helix Group (MD) and Arthur Andersen & Co. (Senior Manager). His academic background was Engineering at Bristol University and his subsequent training was as a Chartered Accountant with Arthur Andersen and Co.

**Lois Brown**

Lois is Vice President of Marketing at Austin Logistics Inc., responsible for brand positioning, marketing communications, and new product definition. Previous experience includes General Manger of Marketing for H. J. Heinz, Inc.; Director of Marketing for Quaker Oats Company; Senior Branding Strategist with LLI-NYC for numerous clients including PepsiCo, Microsoft, and Nabisco; and independent consultant for Silicon Valley start-ups, including Snapfish.com. Lois holds a BA in English and an MBA.

**Jonathan Day**

Jonathan started his career with Citibank working on credit card fraud; he then worked mainly in risk management, with a period in collections management, until leaving the bank in 1989. He then worked as an independent risk management consultant until he joined Statistical Decisions in 1996. He currently manages the Partnership's Greek regional office and, in 2001, was involved in creating a collections company, Europe Matrix, based in Athens.

**Kristopher Fannin**

Kristopher Fannin is President of Intelivate, Inc. Kris has extensive collection and recovery system and decision engine consulting experience in both the telecommunications and finance industries. His background includes IT and system analysis through all development phases of enterprise-wide solutions. Additionally, he has extensive experience in the areas of risk management, recovery and call center consulting, including training for both collection systems and representative skill development.

**Kathy Cole**

Kathy Cole is Marcoms Manager at Intrum Justitia and has several years marketing experience with multi-national organisations using the full marketing mix.

Kathy holds the C.I.M Diploma and is a fully qualified member of the Chartered Institute of Marketing. Her key objective is to provide a full marketing programme for their services and assist with business growth/profit.

**Gordon Crawford**

Gordon was Chief Executive and founder of London Bridge Software which provided credit management based software and consultancy services and was purchased by Fair Isaac in 2004. Gordon has been involved in the computer software industry for over 20 years. After graduating from the University of Newcastle upon Tyne, he spent a number of years in software development, before joining Wang UK Limited in 1982 where he was involved in the management of sales and marketing of the company's hardware and software products to the insurance sector. He left Wang in 1987 to start his own software company.

**Bayan Dekker**
Bayan is the Analytics Director of PIC Solutions. He has over 15 years experience in IT and credit risk management in the retail and financial services industries and has held senior posts at The Foschini Group and Woolworths Financial Services. In his previous positions he has enjoyed the responsibility for credit product development and credit risk management, and has extensive experience with account management and processing systems. He holds a B. Accounting (University of Stellenbosch) and a Diploma in Datametrics (UNISA).

**Donna Guest**
At the time Donna's chapter was written, she was head of Collections at Ventura, a leading UK provider of outsourcing credit management services and a wholly owned subsidiary of Next plc.

**Stephen Holyoake**
Stephen has over 15 years of international credit risk management experience in the retail and finance house environments. He has extensive experience of strategic and operational planning at senior levels and has been responsible for the integration of several collections systems with account management systems from both a technical and operational perspective. He holds an LL.B from the University of Newcastle.

**Margaret Jennion**
Margaret Jennion is a Director of City Consulting Associates, with expertise in insurance, banking and finance. Her specialisation over the last ten years has been consumer finance in the UK and Europe. She previously worked for Merrill Lynch where she was head of Banking Global IT. Before that she worked for seven years with Accenture, having graduated at University College London.

**Stephen Leonard**
Stephen is Managing Director of PIC Solutions. He has over 15 years of risk management experience in the banking and consulting industries at Chase Manhattan Bank and Fair, Isaac International. At Fair, Isaac International he worked in the Europe Middle East Africa Region, consulting on account management, applications processing and scoring projects for clients in the bankcard, retail, current account, personal loans, telecom and mail order arenas. He holds an AS (State University

of New York), BA (University of Toronto), MBA (Adelphi University - School of Banking, New York) and is a member of the UK and SA Institutes of Credit Management.

### Rae Miller

Rae Miller is a Collections Manager at Halifax Bank of Scotland. Prior to HBOS she was a project manager for Attentive (previously known as Lynx Financial Systems). She was responsible for the delivery of Lynx Collections and Recoveries software to customers such as Barclays Bank, Britannia Building Society and Nationwide Building Society. During her career Rae has worked as Collections Policy Manager for Barclays Bank, responsible for the re-design of collections strategies and the implementation of behavioural scorecards. Rae is a graduate member of the ICM.

### Stuart Moseley

Stuart graduated from Southampton University with a BSc Hons in Mathematics and Operational Research in 1994. He has worked for Experian for 10 years latterly as a Business Consultant. Stuart has expertise in the analysis of a variety of scoring solutions implemented for some of the largest financial institutions in the UK. He also has experience in delivering associated strategies and software to integrate solutions into financial institutions systems.

### Martyn Phillips

At the time his chapter was written, Martyn Phillips M.I.C.M. was the Head of Collections and Recovery for the Halifax Bank of Scotland (HBOS) Retail Bank. His chapter seeks to demonstrate the vital importance of effective performance measurement in a high volume retail collections and recovery environment. Many of the arguments, observations and methods apply equally in business-to-business and smaller scale credit management operations.

### Ferdinando Speranza

Nando started his career in banking at Standard Bank Card in 1985, and in 1989 moved to the United Credit Card Division (now ABSA Bank Card). He was a credit manager and for the past five years, a scoring manager. He played an integral part in the successful implementation of both application scoring and behaviour scoring. He currently holds the position of Functional Head, Scoring & Special Projects and is on the verge of completing his MBA.

### Lawrence A. Stineman

Since 1999, Larry Stineman has served as Chief Operating Officer of nDev Technologies, Inc. a global software design and network services company headquartered in Phoenix, Arizona. Prior nDev Technologies, Larry served in a variety of managerial roles at other software development companies and at telecommunications companies including GTE and Fujitsu. Larry attended Loyola University in Chicago, Ill.

### Des Styles

After seven years as the Director of Operations for Associates Capital Corporation in the UK, Des is currently Head of Secured Lending at The funding Corporation. Prior to The Associates, Des spent 15 years with HFC Bank in various operational roles.

### Bob Welsh

Bob Welsh is Head of Debt Management Strategy at the Royal Bank of Scotland. He joined in December 2001 to lead the integration of collection and recovery systems between Royal Bank and NatWest and to develop combined strategy going forward. Prior to that Bob was at the Bank of Scotland Group for 17 years, latterly as Head of Debt Management Services. A member of the Institute of Credit Management and American Collector's Association, Bob has some 30 years experience in Risk and Debt Management.

# INDEX

## A

Abandoned call · 54
Action-specific · 183
Activity Based Costing · 103
Agent contribution · 46
Attrition scores · 207, 208
Automatic Call Handling · 14, 30, 147, 168, 183, 186
Awards · 41, 42, 43

## B

Behavioural scoring · 32, 106, 127, 151, 152, 155, 179
Best practice · 19, 21, 24, 27, 28, 30, 57, 86, 168, 187, 198, 199, 200, 202, 203, 207, 209, 210

## C

Call centre · 46, 70
Call quality · 53, 54
Capacity planning · 6, 62, 63, 64, 127
Centralised · 9, 10, 12, 25
Champion/challenger · 32, 63, 118, 138, 188, 195, 196, 215, 216, 217, 218, 219
Chronological Analysis · 129
Churn · 26, 115
Collections scorecard · 62, 151, 158, 159, 191, 193
Contact efficiency · 48, 50
Cradle to grave · 11

Credit bureau · 164, 171, 173, 183, 205, 206, 207
Credit card · 5, 6, 77, 110, 120, 133, 137, 181, 188, 214, 217, 224
CRM · 180, 187, 207, 209
Current account · 76, 120, 134, 137
Customer centric · 221, 224
Customer scoring · 225

## D

Data Protection · 53, 78, 80
Davox · 116
Decision tree · 14, 15, 17, 18, 21, 195
Dialler · 221
Dunning · 59, 194
Dynamic delinquency report · 130

## E

Employee hours · 46
Excel · 99
External audit · 74, 76, 79

## I

Inbound · 46, 63, 70, 116, 121, 194
In-sourcing · 67
Internal audit · 74, 75, 77, 79, 80, 81, 82

# K

Kept promise · 45, 51, 53, 56

# L

Litigation · 55, 68, 138
Loan · 65, 68, 69, 105, 114, 120

# M

Management Information Systems ·
    117, 118, 120, 121
Markov Chains · 94, 98, 99
Melita · 116
Middleware · 222
Money · 4, 28, 34, 35, 36, 38, 39, 40,
    43, 48, 52, 55, 80, 86, 100, 101, 106,
    148, 177, 178, 181, 184, 186, 187,
    188
Months on book · 210
MORI · 133
Mortgage · 3, 76, 79, 110, 221, 222
Mosaix · 116
Motivation · 33, 36, 37, 43, 62, 71, 101,
    127, 186
Motivational Map · 34, 35
Motor finance · 129

# N

Negotiation · 8, 38, 45, 51, 68, 125
Net roll rates · 92, 94

# O

Odds · 101, 107, 166, 168, 169, 172,
    202, 207
Outbound · 46, 50, 59, 63, 70, 116, 117,
    121, 147, 217
Outcome Period · 159, 160, 161, 195
Outsourcing · 43, 59, 67, 83, 84, 85, 86,
    87, 88, 89, 111, 112
Overdraft · 77

# P

P&L · 4, 5, 72, 75, 76, 77
Performance definition · 165
Personal loan · 65, 133
Planning · 7, 45, 64, 66, 67, 69, 71, 72
Policy groups · 13, 23
Power dialling · 196
Pre-dialling · 120
Predictive dialling · 117
Profile · 25, 31, 41, 62, 97, 131, 168,
    169, 200, 201
Profiles · 16, 29, 97, 98, 168, 169, 170,
    188, 199, 200, 201, 203, 204
Promise kept · 45, 51, 53, 56
Promise to pay · 45, 48, 51, 52, 125,
    137
Proportional cost · 215
Provision · 5, 29, 37, 48, 49, 50, 75,
    130, 147

# R

Recession · 7, 8, 125
Recoveries · 1, 3, 5, 47, 55, 76, 108,
    111, 130, 134, 135, 137, 138
Regression · 175, 183, 185, 188
Repossession · 3, 68, 80, 130
ROI · 113, 114
Roll rate · 7, 77, 92, 93, 94, 95, 96, 97,
    99, 112, 130, 139, 160, 161, 215,
    218, 219, 220

# S

Salary · 72
Script · 19, 38
Segmentation · 10, 13, 14, 18, 20, 62,
    81, 109, 205, 211, 212, 213
Service levels · 199
Settlement · 8, 183
SMART · 50
Specialisation · 10, 11
Staff development · 223
Structure · 9, 29, 37, 39, 40, 63, 71, 73,
    122
Sub-population · 156, 158, 159, 160

# *T*

Timing · 17, 199, 202, 217
Tone · 15, 16, 17, 19, 81, 125
Trace · 11, 55, 80, 212, 213
Tracking · 48, 51, 54, 64, 99, 113, 122
Training · 9, 23, 40, 41, 43, 45, 51, 54,
    61, 71, 72, 79, 84, 114, 125
Transition matrix · 93, 94, 99
True Negatives · 206
True Positives · 206
True roll rates · 92, 93, 94
Type · 14, 16, 17, 19, 51, 55, 60, 67,
    70, 108, 142, 152, 159, 175, 185,
    186, 195, 208, 210

# *V*

Validation · 144
Value at risk · 195
Vanson Bourne · 133
Virtual call centre · 146, 147

# *W*

Wages · 66
Welbeck Finance · 125